DEVELOPING
A
CONSULTING
PRACTICE

S U R V I V A L   S K I L L S   F O R   S C H O L A R S

Managing Editor: Mitchell Allen

Survival Skills for Scholars provides you, the professor or advanced graduate student working in a college or university setting, with practical suggestions for making the most of your academic career. These brief, readable guides will help you with skills that you are required to master as a college professor but may have never been taught in graduate school. Using hands-on, jargon-free advice and examples, forms, lists, and suggestions for additional resources, experts on different aspects of academic life give invaluable tips on managing the day-to-day tasks of academia—effectively and efficiently.

Volumes in This Series

SURVIVAL SKILLS FOR SCHOLARS

DEVELOPING A CONSULTING PRACTICE

ROBERT O. METZGER

SAGE Publications
International Educational and Professional Publisher
Newbury Park   London   New Delhi

To Dorothee, My Wife, My Proofreader
Lo, These 25 Years

Copyright © 1993 by Sage Publications, Inc.

For information address:

SAGE Publications, Inc.
2455 Teller Road
Newbury Park, California 91320

SAGE Publications Ltd.
6 Bonhill Street
London EC2A 4PU
United Kingdom

SAGE Publications India Pvt. Ltd.
M-32 Market
Greater Kailash I
New Delhi 110 048 India

Printed in the United States of America

Library of Congress Cataloging-in-Publication Data

Main entry under title:

Metzger, Robert O.
    Developing a consulting practice / Robert O. Metzger.
        p.   cm.   — (Survival skills for scholars ; vol. 3)
    Includes bibliographical references.
    ISBN 0-8039-5046-2 (cl.). — ISBN 0-8039-5047-0 (pbk.)
    1. Consultants—Vocational guidance. 2. Scholars—Vocational
guidance. 3. Research—Vocational guidance. I. Title.
II. Series.
HD69.C6M468   1993
001'.068—dc20   93-24840
                                                            CIP

93 94 95 96   10 9 8 7 6 5 4 3 2 1

Sage Production Editor: Yvonne Könneker

Contents

1 | You Wanna Do What?

Genesis

The practice of consulting probably dates back to when Mog was sitting in the cave and asked Grog, the best flint maker in the tribe, for help flaking flint stones. Mog certainly had to pay Grog with a piece of meat or a half dozen arrowheads or whatever, but consulting was born!

As we enter the 21st century, consulting is a respected avocation performed by most scholars at one time or another in their career by way of sharing their research findings and expertise with entities not connected with their college or university, usually private enterprises, research centers, or nonprofit institutions. However, such consultation cannot be thought of exclusively as business school professors working for and with Fortune 1000 company executives. In fact, consulting today has an enormous range from the geographer providing assistance to, say, Rand-McNally or the National Geographic Society to psychologists providing counsel to family-owned and -managed businesses trying to deal with family strife, to music scholars and scholars of antiquity providing assistance to PBS in the development of some of that network's special programs.

This book attempts to address the *content* consultation process (see Schein, 1969) as performed by scholars in all fields

1

interested in developing their consultative skills and activities into a business. It may be a for-profit activity to supplement their academic income or it may be a nonprofit endeavor focused on developing action research projects or case studies for the classroom. Or it may be to develop their consultative skills in the management of their organization within academe or an independent research facility, but whatever the ultimate purpose, consulting as the focus of this book is to *be performed as a regular activity and managed as a business.*

Furthermore, although this effort spans all manners of formalized consulting, most consulting is for profit and is considered *management* consulting. As a result, much of the text will address issues of management consulting as a model for all consulting efforts, whether evaluating antique furniture before auction or providing psychological motivation to dieters with special weight problems.

The idea for the book emerged from a preconference workshop I have been holding for colleagues at the National Academy of Management for the past 10 years. As a member of the executive committee of the Managerial Consultation Division, I was asked by Achilles Armenakis at Auburn to provide a program for scholars interested in starting or expanding their efforts outside their academic work and for graduate students who still had not decided if they wanted to enter teaching or research; or, if they wanted to take the expertise gained from their graduate studies to develop a full-time professional practice. The original program drew heavily on the heuristics of my own 25 years of consulting work and from teaching management consulting skills in the MBA track at the University of Southern California School of Business Administration in the 1980s. The workshop became an extraordinary success, and scholars young and old, doctoral students, psychologists, scientists from government and industry, and many experienced consultants attended year after year.

Over time the original workshop content was modified, primarily in response to the most frequently asked questions from the audience. The format of this book allows me to include a series of diagrams of various conceptual models and samples of worksheets, checklists, and documents to support the dialogue.

Imparting Wisdom

If there is wisdom to impart to you, it is this: Consulting as a process and a professional service evolves around humanity's folly and the uncertainties and insecurities inherent in managing any large organization of people. The role the consultant must play is to look past the obvious symptoms to recognize and identify the root cause of the mismanagement and then to develop solutions that call for dysfunctional behavioral and value modifications that are acceptable to the perpetrators!

What is often startling to my audience about this definition is that it has little to do with the scholarship or self-anointed technical expertise we assume generates the consulting assignment, whereas it has a great deal to do with psychology, human motivation, effective communication, and deeply emotional issues such as trust, respect, passion, and ego. If this sounds more like a televised soap opera, it has all the makings.

People are asked for a variety of reasons to manage a business or some nonprofit institution. More often than not, such people believe they have reached such heights before they are ready, and the trouble begins when they start to worry about looking good. They exist not to be found out! It is all downhill from there.

People in managerial roles will not delegate lest they be held accountable for others' mistakes. They will not share information lest others conceptualize solutions better than their own. They will not change their methods and values lest they look bad in front of their peers. All of this culminates in an environment described some years ago by Kübler-Ross in her brilliant treatise on the stages experienced by terminally ill patients. The first are *self-denial* and *isolation*, the terminally ill keep to themselves and do not communicate their distress or admit that something is amiss ("Whadaya mean we're losing market share?"). This is followed by *anger* ("Why me, Lord?"). *Bargaining* follows in the form of prayers or letters to one's representative in Congress for that extra trade tariff bill. Finally, *depression* sets in, which is followed by *acceptance*. And a stage at which all consultants find they face similar issues, regardless of their field of expertise, is in getting their clients from denial to acceptance in the shortest period of time with the least amount of damage to themselves, others, or the organization.

This translates in the real world to George, an acknowledged researcher and scholar in marketing niche exploitation, who is asked to help with a marketing problem only to find that Sales will not listen to Production, which is trying to communicate that they are selling widgets faster than the factory can make them. And the finance department is trying to get someone to listen to the fact that they are selling the widgets for below cost. Meanwhile, the boss won't listen to anyone about developing a strategic plan for a company operating in an industry in which the paradigm and the products are changing every 5 years. And poor George thought he was being hired for his research abilities!

This hypothetical example is meant to focus on the reality that whatever our special expertise, more often than not, we are hired as consultants to solve human, not functional or technical problems. This leads to the point that consulting scholars need to develop a broad range of skills that go far beyond their discrete academic fields. However, it also opens up opportunities to help managers grow and mature, improve the functionality of complex organizations, and generate solutions to a broad range of problems being experienced by multiple stakeholders. It's a lot of fun, and you can make some money doing it. Just don't limit your self-image to being an expert *only* in antiquities, psychology, or accounting.

The Principal Consultative Skills

One of the more constant discussions that occur among consulting scholars concerns the attributes and skills required to transfer the scholar's unique knowledge and insights in their chosen field to that of successful consultation, that is, to providing a service that addresses the needs of the client. A major impetus of these arguments wells up from several dangerous assumptions that some find easy to make about consulting.

The first such assumption is that clients will beat a path to your door just because of what you know as a leading expert in your field. Who's going to tell them? Few people outside academia read any of the scholarly journals in which we tend to publish, and those that do occasionally read these esoteric articles do not understand that we are writing primarily as an act of scholarship and for the benefit of our peers. Certainly, they do not understand the statistical proofs or the implications of the data developed from pure research. Furthermore, few potential clients realize how our specialized knowledge can and should be applied to their day-to-day problems. Most business people have a very confused, if not thoroughly negative, concept of academics and researchers. As a result, unless you take the initiative and rework your scholarly articles to fit the editorial style and content of more popular periodicals and republish them where you will get exposure to the consulting marketplace, no one will ever be aware of you. But this issue goes much further than just reworking a few articles, it also includes learning how to network, make practical presentations to industry and public groups, write timely op-ed columns, and make public presentations that provide high exposure. These issues will be addressed in detail in Chapter 2.

A second assumption that scholars make all too often is that the skills required to become a successful management consultant are the same as those of a successful executive. Some attributes of effective executives are similar to those needed by effective consultants; however, there are some obvious differences that must be taken into consideration. First, consultants do not have the authority required to implement their recommendations. They do not command the resources of the client organization and frequently are asked to install their solutions in the face of overt organizational resistance. To the contrary, effective consultants have to be as effective as executives and also be able to accomplish even more with few, if any, organizational resources. Easy to conceptualize, very difficult to achieve.

A third assumption is that all you need to know and bring to the client is your expertise in your field. Again, nothing could be further from the truth! In addition to your unique knowledge in your field, you are expected to bring along a number of skills from objectivity in diagnosing root problems to creativity in developing and implementing solutions, especially when those solutions are not popular. Besides being a scholarly expert, you are expected to be an effective change agent, economic clairvoyant, and industry visionary. Being an Eagle Scout is much easier and a fairer expectation.

This chapter, then, highlights the critical skills required to be an effective consultant, based on my personal experience over a period of 25 years as well as interviews with other successful scholars in regard to their efforts as consultants. In an earlier text Greiner and I (1982) identified seven specific skills areas full-time consultants must develop if they are to succeed in the profession. Each is equally applicable for consulting scholars. These skills are (a) diagnostic ability, (b) implementation skills, (c) specialized knowledge, (d) communication and presentation skills, (e) marketing and sales skills, (f) managerial skills, and (g) other individual attributes supportive of consulting. When talking with clients about how and why they use consultants, I frequently hear that consultants also are expected to be poised, credible, and professional. Unfortunately, these simple labels belie the range of underlying skills that combine to make an effective consultant. And, from my own experience, I would add a passion for problem solving and a real desire to help other people as two very critical characteristics one must have to be a successful consultant. Let's discuss each of these issues briefly.

Diagnostic Ability

Any scholar spending the briefest amount of time with professional consultants will learn that, more often than not, ills described by clients are only symptoms of deeper issues. It is the ability of consultants to look beyond the obvious, to remain objective about the issues, regardless of what the client claims, until root causes are discovered and understood. It is this ability to be a true diagnostician that separates the very successful consultant from the marginal one.

And, this *ability to remain objective* is particularly challenging for scholars who are often the personification of the old saw: If all you have to work with is a hammer, every problem looks like a nail. For scholars, frequently every problem looks like it needs their unique perspective regardless of the issues. Communications specialists find it temptingly easy to see everything as a communications issue, compensation experts tend to look at everything as soluble with compensation adjustments, and finance specialists want to see everything fixed with additional financial analysis. So a prime skills set needed by consulting scholars is a broader understanding of the issues faced by client organizations and an ability to diagnose the issues beyond one's scholarly field of knowledge when that is appropriate. The art historian who realizes when a paleontologist is needed to help address an issue is far more valuable to the client museum than any purist art history scholar.

Within this broad skill area, I would add *curiosity* to that of objectivity. The really fine consultants are immensely curious to learn new information about their general field, be it business or health care, executive education or social issues. Full-time consultants relish the opportunity to serve a client in a new industry or with problems in other fields so long as they believe that they really can help. Clients, in turn, value consultants who become intellectually challenged by their business, their problems, and the issues confronting their industry. Without strong curiosity, a consultant becomes very narrow in his or her experience and ability to help clients.

A third diagnostic skill required of consulting scholars is *analytical*, or the ability to understand issues on a broad scale. For example, although you may have diagnosed the root cause of the client's trauma, does the issue stop there: Is it an isolated problem or is the cause a systemic one that permeates the client's organization across all divisions and plants? This ability to spot patterns in issues is critical for effective consulting, too.

Problem-Solving Skills

Yet another dangerous assumption by consulting scholars is that all they need do is share their specialist knowledge with the client to resolve the problem. This is just not true. It is one thing to define a problem, to identify its root cause, or to bring new information and knowledge to bear to provide a fresh perspective, but clients also need help thinking through what the best remedial action may be and what steps to take to begin the change process while implementing a solution. Good consultants bring these skills to bear, too. It's one thing to claim you are a fire department by running around crying "Fire!" every time you see smoke. It is something else altogether to stick around and actually help put the fire out. And, within that, to build a relationship whereby the client asks you to stay and help put it out.

Imagination goes hand in hand with problem-solving skills. Often the greatest service a consultant provides to a client is a perspective, a slant, a bias, that has never been perceived from within the client's paradigm. This ability to be a creative problem solver is crucial to long-term success as a consulting scholar. *Courage* also travels well with creative problem solving, because often new ideas and perspectives can be very threatening to a client and the client's organization. As a result, your courage, your strength of conviction in your diagnosis of the problem, and your solution may be the only thing standing in support of your ideas. For scholars, though, this is nothing new. Many of us have had the experience of proposing and defending new and unpopular ideas—ideas that flew in the face of conventional wisdom—that resulted from our research. And it has only been through courage and strength of conviction that the research and the new ideas have persevered. Consulting is no different, and anyone who tells you it is easy, has never worked on any significant project.

Finally, I would add *teaching ability* to this area of consulting skills. Effective consultants are invariably very good, if not natural, teachers. For no matter how brilliant your diagnosis or the creativity of your solutions, if you cannot help the client learn how to manage the required change process to implement your solutions, you will not be a success as a consultant. Furthermore, the teaching skills required are executive education skills rather than classroom teaching skills. Executives, managers, and supervisors prefer to hear about concrete, practical examples and successes. The theories and concepts behind them are nowhere near as important in working with managers as they are in the undergraduate classroom.

Specialized Knowledge

There is no question that as a consulting scholar you are being hired to provide your unique knowledge and perspective on the issues at hand. But how ephemeral are that data or your most recent theories? Is your specialized knowledge up-to-date? Does it reflect the true outer envelope of thinking in your field? For the most part that is what your client thinks he or she is hiring and expects your work to be that current. If all you are doing is packaging your 5-year-old research data in a new wrapper, you cannot and should not be trying to sell yourself as a knowledge-based consultant. Scholars who rest on their earlier research efforts do not last long as consultants posing as leading thinkers or specialists.

Furthermore, your specialized knowledge is of little value to your client if you are unable to apply that knowledge in practical ways to address the client's needs. For example, it is one thing to perform research that helps to define what employees really want in the way of fringe benefits from their employer. But it is an altogether different task to develop those benefits into an easily understood and administered program that the client's employees can manage and administer for themselves. Often, the client is hiring you to provide more of the latter and less of the former. But you will not be serving the client well unless you are able and prepared to do both aspects of the work. Just providing theory or research data is not enough when it comes to specialized knowledge.

Communication Skills

Listening skills seem to top the list of communications skills required by consulting scholars. Frequently, interviews with client principals generate as much or more valuable information and facts for defining problems and developing solutions as any other source of data, including questionnaires and attitudinal surveys. However, the effectiveness of the interview and the robustness of the information surfaced from those interviews are predicated on the consultant's listening skills. This usually means listening beyond the obvious to identify what has *not* been said in response to a particular line of inquiry. This would include the ability to formulate followup questions that break through convention and provide information truly relevant to the issues.

Writing and presentation skills also are critical here. Developing an effective proposal of work; presenting clear, well-thought-out interim reports for the client; designing and developing final reports, or more common, audiovisual presentations of findings, conclusions, and recommendations are all critical consulting duties. *Oratory skills,* too, play an important part in the development of a successful consulting style. Life is often nothing more than an endless series of arguments about the value of your beliefs and the data from which you develop your conclusions. It was true when you chose your dissertation topic, when you presented your research, and when you wrote your dissertation, and it will continue to be true when you are a consulting scholar, continuously challenged to help your client understand your perspective and be motivated to take your advice.

Finally, in the area of communication skills, it is fundamental that you develop your *intervention skills*. As mentioned above, clients often expect much more from you as a consulting scholar than just your unique technical knowledge and understanding of your field. Clients also expect you to help them design useful solutions and to help implement those solutions. Clients are very good in running their businesses on a day-to-day basis. It is altogether different when asking them to manage change. They are not skilled in it and need a change agent, someone with strong implementation skills, to help resolve the problems identified. Often, these intervention skills will consist of little more than the ability to design and deliver a training program. However, occasionally they also will require your ability and skill to act as arbiter, judge, or facilitator.

Marketing and Selling Abilities

Without a client, you don't have a consulting practice. To develop clients and meet your objectives in the consulting profession, scholars also need marketing and selling skills. But this area of competence goes beyond the simple statement of fact; you must truly enjoy marketing and selling, honing the skills required to convince others of your point of view—that you are the best person to address the problems or issues at hand and that your ideas and recommendations are the most practical resolutions to those situations.

Again, this is nothing new! You have been doing it since the day you started your doctoral project: every time you responded to a student's challenge in the classroom, and each day you tried to present new ideas to your department chair or dean. But marketing your consulting services is even more challenging than selling your ideas to friends and colleagues on a daily, if not hourly, basis. It goes beyond doing it—you have to *enjoy* doing it while developing a thick skin. Selling your consulting services in the open marketplace against other full-time professional consulting organizations is a very humbling experience, one that consists of a great deal of rejection. It is a process that tends to make prima donnas humble and scholars realistic. It also is a process that will drive out anyone who tends to personalize the volume of rejection. Gaining a client through the marketing of your consulting services is a numbers game. You will talk with a dozen people. Four will express sincere interest and ask for a proposal. Occasionally, one of those proposals will be accepted and turn into a client relationship. And there is no ground rule that says each gaggle of prospects will lead to one job. To the contrary, you may have to go through 100 prospects and write 50 proposals before one is accepted. That adds up to a great deal of rejection, lost time, and utter frustration. It's a hard thing to learn to love! Chapters 2 and 3 go into great detail on both indirect and direct methods for marketing your consulting services, but none of that advice will help you if you don't enjoy the thrill of the hunt and the challenge of debate!

Business Sense

Another principal skill consulting scholars must have to succeed in building a practice is that of a *business sense*. By this I mean the ability to understand and design a personal strategy for your consulting effort; a sensitivity of what it takes to build and maintain a successful business enterprise; a general knowledge of the principles of business law, contracts, marketing, and selling; and the skill to act as a manager, tutor, and supervisor—from directing a team of researchers to guiding an internal task force within the client's organization to managing the employees of your own business.

Unless your field is that of business administration, these skills can only be developed over time through trial and error and discussion with other consulting scholars. All of the above expertise requires knowledge and understanding about a broad range of issues outside your area of scholarly expertise. Yet it is these additional skills that will be the platform on which you will develop and enlarge your consulting practice. A successful consulting effort is not a hobby or something to be attempted in any evanescent way—it is the design and direction of a business, one built on your scholarship and unique knowledge and experiences.

Personal Traits

From my own experience and that of my peers, from providing counsel to major consulting organizations, and through reading a number of books written in the past decade about the consulting profession, I have discovered that there is a rainbow of personal traits and characteristics that most knowledgeable people, and especially clients, expect or assume are an integral part of the consultants they hire. I will cover them briefly, although each is worth its own monograph.

Empathy. The ability to relate to your client and his or her issues of concern is vital. Although the problem may seem to be merely an intellectual exercise to most scholars, a consulting scholar also must be highly sensitive to the pain and consternation the situation brings to the client's organization or family or peers. Empathy is also required in large doses in recognizing the trauma imposed by whatever changes may be required to implement needed solutions to the problems at hand. Without such empathy, a consultant will not always define the problem effectively or propose realistic solutions in regard to the constraints faced by the client.

Energy. The demands and challenges of the profession can be fueled only with extraordinary levels of energy—energy to be a self-starter, never to tire in the face of what may appear to be endless rejection, to possess the strength and patience required to develop a solid working relationship with a new client, and to persevere and sell your solutions and implement change. And for the consulting scholar, this energy is in addition to that required for routine research and teaching responsibilities back at school! Deciding to begin a consulting effort is a major decision for a scholar, one that cannot be easily commenced or, once begun, abandoned.

Ethics. Of all the characteristics consultants are assumed to have, ethics is prime. In this age, ethics covers a very broad spread of issues, from keeping client confidences, to respecting client relationships, to being fair about fees and expenses billed, to making recommendations that can affect individual careers and lives. Clients often treat their consultant as they would a parish priest, and the consultant must know what level of ethical responsibility that relationship infers.

Positive Thinking. Along with energy, positive thinking and a positive attitude are fundamental to successful consulting. Much of a consultant's success rests in the ability to be optimistic, to be a self-starter, and to act as a role model for clients in the face of apparently hopeless situations. It is this ability to find a way around the normal paradigm of problem definition and resolution, to fight off discouraging situations and events, that separates successful and effective consultants from those who are only partially committed.

Self-Motivation. Whether it is an issue of continuing to knock on doors to secure a new client, of writing yet another proposal to a prospect who did not buy the first three you sent, of getting up a half hour earlier to do that needed research, or of preparing effective handouts for the day's meetings, effective consultants find the energy and strength they need inside themselves—nowhere else.

Team Player. Although most consulting scholars operate solo practices, do not take on partners, and never expand their practice beyond what they can handle in the way of workload and commitment, the only successful consulting scholars are those who understand and enjoy being team players—with the client, with the client's organization, with other consultants who may be working with the client on other projects, with other scholars knowledgeable about the issues or the problem, and with peers back at school. No consultant, no matter what his or her reputation, achieved any real success being a loner or an eccentric. They all are team players, scholars who enjoy sharing and working with others. Scholars unable to do this consistently and effectively have little future claiming to be consultants.

Self-Fulfillment. Consulting is a thankless activity. Certainly a successful consulting scholar can add $100,000 or more to his or her income by consulting on a fairly regular basis, but clients rarely ever call to say how good they feel as a result of your work. Few, if any, will ever write you a letter for your career file stating that they continue in business solely as a result of what you did for them. Unlike academia, where letters of thanks and certificates of recognition are a major source of fulfillment and reward, consulting does not provide any fulfillment other than monetary and that which can be self-generated. It is in knowing what you have accomplished for the client that is all that your psyche should need—that, the fees, and the experience. Because, the minute the project is over and you are gone, the client presents your ideas to the board as his or her own, the plan you developed for them appears in the annual report over the chairman's name and your contributions go unheralded. If you are considering consulting as a form of recognition, forget it! That will come in other, less direct ways.

Mobility. Mobility and, certainly, flexibility are key characteristics any consulting scholar must possess or develop. Even those trying to consult close to home may find themselves being asked to visit this plant or that sales region to develop good data or obtain different perspectives about the issues. And, from time to time, you may receive a call or a fax from the other side of the country or the globe asking for your counsel and advice. No matter how much you may detest traveling, it is pretty heady stuff—the kind that builds professional reputations. Flexibility also is a critical trait. Often the problem will turn out to be something other than what the client said it would be, or the client likes your solution to the problem but cannot use your implementation plan, or some other delay will crop up testing the patience of a saint! Throughout it all, the consultant is expected to remain calm, dedicated, concerned, empathetic, and very, very flexible. The terms and conditions of the client far outweigh the terms and conditions of the consultant; consulting scholars who insist on consulting only on their own terms and conditions before they have earned a reputation don't get a great deal of opportunity to practice their avocation.

Having reviewed some of the major talents and traits effective consultants need to succeed, let's move on to what it takes to get a client and begin a consulting career.

2 | Indirect Marketing Strategies

Like an actor without a role, as a consulting scholar you are nothing until you have a client, and unless you know the way to the Fountain of Youth, few if any prospective clients will ever beat a path to your door! Stated as directly as possible, you must make concerted, ongoing efforts to let the marketplace know you are offering your services and you need to make the market knowledgeable about your special areas of interest, research, and knowledge—so much so that prospective clients feel sufficiently intrigued to call you.

What Is Indirect Marketing?

There are two fundamental ways to market your consulting services: *directly*, by knocking on doors, and *indirectly*, via a broad range of third-party media and means. This chapter and the next two are designed to provide you with a wealth of ideas about how you can market your consulting services, directly and indirectly, and prepare and deliver proposals that will bring you consulting projects. This chapter deals with indirect marketing, which is the least objectionable path scholars choose to take when promoting themselves and their services.

For the first three-quarters of the 20th century, management consulting services were promoted primarily through *indirect* methods. It was considered unprofessional for full-time consultants or leading consulting and accounting firms to market via hard-sell methods or advertising their services. As a result, the major CPA partnerships such as Arthur Andersen, Coopers & Lybrand, and Price, Waterhouse together with the premier consulting firms such as McKinsey & Company would rent the most prestigious office space in major cities, encourage their principals and partners to join the United Way, the Boy Scouts of America, the local Harvard Business School Club, and of course, the best private business and country clubs. Through the development of high-powered networks, by rubbing elbows daily with the senior executives of leading area firms, by delivering speeches, and by contributing heavily to local charities, these senior consultants would permeate the business community and generate consulting assignments. Furthermore, based on their extensive investments in bright young MBAs, researchers, and significant libraries of data, research projects of interest to various industries would be carried out and the results published in business journals and newspapers such as *The Wall Street Journal*. All generated enough interest for curious executives to call for more data and information.

Over time, these efforts paid off handsomely and went a long way toward creating the fine reputations such firms continue to enjoy to this day. The operative phrase, however, is *over time*, because indirect marketing efforts require a great deal of time and significant financial resources and cash flow from existing clients to pay all those expensive people for months, and even years, before they lead to work. And there is always the risk that with so many partners and principals in high-profile positions throughout the community, one ethical, moral, or human error could undo everything the rest had worked years to accomplish, toward establishing a solid firm reputation.

Indirect Strategies for Scholars

Unfortunately for scholars and especially for academics eager to start a new consulting practice and, for that matter, most smaller consulting firms, one cannot possibly afford to try these kinds of costly indirect marketing methods. However, there are a number of indirect marketing ploys you can try—in fact I would advise you to try all of them simultaneously, if you are serious about starting a successful practice. These efforts include performing industry-based research, rewriting and publishing your key journal articles in the leading industry and business periodicals, delivering speeches and papers at industry-sponsored conferences and conventions, providing interviews to your regional media as a local or campus expert, writing op-ed columns for the local or national newspapers, and informing your university administrative networks that you are available for and interested in consulting. We will explore each of these in turn.

Designing Targeted Research

Most of the research we perform for academic and peer credit tends to be esoteric in relationship to what laypeople and business executives want and need in the way of knowledge. Much of our research and our hypotheses are of little practical value in the everyday world. The good news is that we are skilled at designing and performing research, our graduate students need projects, and surprise, surprise, many local client firms will help fund research projects that are of real interest to them. My doctoral dissertation, titled *Organizational Issues to Strategic Planning in the Commercial Banking Industry*, was based on just such a research project and was funded entirely by the Bank Administration Institute in Chicago.

The first step, then, in developing such projects is to focus on your field, discipline, or a particular industry to determine what business executives and lay leaders in that arena feel they need to know. It may turn out that what they really *want* to know is not what they *need* to know, but who ever said commercially based research was an exercise in truth?

So let's say you are interested in the insurance industry. You have called a number of insurance companies and interviewed senior executives, and they tend to want to know whether left-handed people buy more annuities than right-handed people. (Deep stuff!) One company even inferred that they would be willing to support such a research effort. On this basis you design a project. It is important to determine if your audience wants the data locally, regionally, nationally, or internationally.

Another research ploy frequently used by leading consulting firms is to develop a questionnaire concerning some sensitive issue in an industry, let's say executive pay, and then to send the questionnaire out to all the leading firms in the industry with a cover letter to the CEOs stating that if their companies will participate in the survey, you will send them a free copy of the results, coded in such a way that they can identify their own specifics—but not necessarily their competitors'— and the industry means and averages.

Having completed your survey or market/attitudinal research, the next critical step is to interpret the data not so much from the perspective of a scholar as from the perspective of an executive in that industry. What do the data tell managers? How might managers use the results to improve their business, sales, morale, or organizational effectiveness? If more research is needed, what should the study entail and what hypotheses might be tested as a result? Or how do the data apply to family-owned and -managed businesses or to non-profit institutions? The more you can role-play the mind of the industry executive, the more effective your project will be in gaining you a solid, industry-based reputation.

Finally, identify the industry publications that most leading executives read on a monthly or quarterly basis. Call the editor and ask his or her guidance in outlining an executive-oriented article that presents the results of your research. Of course, if a client company or an industry grant has paid you for the research, be sure to clear the article with your sponsor before it is published. Let the sponsor know you want everyone in the industry to share in the results. Rarely will a sponsor ask you to withhold such an article.

One additional step in this research-based, indirect process of marketing your consulting services and expertise is to draft a story based on the research results for the business section of your local newspaper. If the study is sufficiently newsworthy or the results of interest to a wider audience, there is nothing preventing you from submitting a "special to *The New York Times*," or whichever paper would give you national prominence.

Here is just one of many examples from my own experience: Toward the end of the 1970s, Congress was in the process of modifying banking regulations to permit banks and savings and loan companies to offer a much broader array of personal investment and financial services products. The bad news was that bankers had no idea which products or services to develop under these new authorities. And this was critical information to have, because many large banks were contemplating the expense of millions of dollars to acquire other financial service companies to be able to offer those products and services exclusively.

In the midst of all this turmoil and uncertainty, I suggested to one of my clients, a prestigious, upscale private bank in a very affluent southern California community, that they allow me to design and perform some customer-based research to determine what, if anything, its retail customers really wanted as a result of the new regulations. The client agreed and funded a major study that, over the ensuing 4 months, provided some of the most robust data ever developed on this subject in the industry.

The results were really quite interesting. I will just summarize that what the very wealthy really wanted, so the data showed, was better personalized service, period. In fact, they did not perceive that their banker could develop credible expertise in insurance, brokerage services, or tax management overnight. Most of these depositors already had such relationships with other specialists anyway. Needless to say, these results had immensely important implications for any banker intending to invest significant sums of capital in the development of new, nontraditional services for their upscale customers. (Another way of stating all this is that my co-researcher and I got lucky!)

After we provided the data and our interpretations to the client bank, we asked the bank president if he had any problem with our developing an article about the research and our findings for a leading banking journal. He said no, with the proviso that we disguise the identity of the bank and the region of the country where the work was performed, for competitive reasons.

The article appeared about 6 months later in *The Journal of Retail Banking,* and we were able to place related articles in selected newspapers around the same time that the journal article was published. All of this led to several years of additional related work with a number of other financial institutions. The journal article appeared as that issue's lead piece together with a similar research study performed on the East Coast based on middle-class depositors of a large, chain bank. That, in turn, did not hurt our academic standing. We received credit and recognition for the article even though it was not a pure academic piece. And we were cited in *The Congressional Record* by the Senate Banking and Finance Committee as a result of the implications of our findings on the industry. All this stemmed from a suggestion to a client to fund some research!

Publishing and Republishing

As mentioned earlier, laypeople and business executives do not read our scholarly journals. When one of them does, he or she finds our style and methods confusing and esoteric and swears never to try reading statistical research again! This leads the consulting scholar to two opportunities: reworking his or her publications for lay audiences in popular business periodicals and interpreting the most challenging work of colleagues for specific industry executives (with permission, of course).

Even business journals such as the *Harvard Business Review, The California Management Review,* and *Sloan Management Review* are seldom perused by managers or business leaders. First, they simply do not allocate enough time in their schedules to read. Second, the material that they do read is addressed to their unique industry or organizational needs—pragmatic solutions to pressing problems. A few scholars and prolific consultants—such as Levinson and Argyris of Harvard, Bennis of the University of Southern California, and of course, Drucker at Claremont—write directly to this audience and have become cultural gurus of the business world for decades. However, each year there is a score of very fine, thoughtful articles published by scholars that could be immensely helpful to managers and executives if their ideas and conclusions were adapted to specific industry issues or cultural business problems. Simply put, if you have good ideas based on solid research, then you should be developing two articles for every one you conceptualize. The first, naturally, should be for peer review and academic credit, but then you should develop a second article that applies your findings and thinking to specific, worldly issues. One way to find the key to this approach is to collaborate with a successful consulting firm in your area. Talk with consultants who deal with business issues daily. You may even invite one of the principals of the firm to be your coauthor. Another good source for ways to apply your research is your own clients. Ask them how your ideas might be useful within their industry and organization.

We each read dozens of articles monthly by our peers that also present formidable ideas if only they could be translated into lay terms and explained relative to specific business and industry problems. Taking those ideas that address very specific topical issues, reworking the original premise to address those issues, and doing so while providing full credit to the original scholar's work, you can help your consulting effort immensely. Examples in my own career abound. Although I have always developed lay versions of my own academic articles for publication in industry periodicals, I also have modified the work of others—for example, that of Jemison at Texas on mergers and acquisitions for the financial services industry, that of Chase and Wheelwright on quality issues in manufacturing adopted to service industries, and that of Clark and Pratt in London on organizational life cycles as applicable to the savings and loan crisis of a few years ago—to develop articles that managers and executives can use to apply to immediate industry issues. This does not mean that I plagiarize or in any way suggest that plagiarism be used. To the contrary, in every case, I prominently attributed the concept and research to the scholars who performed it, most often right at the start of my article, and I do so continually throughout such articles. But it has been the understanding of a particular industry and business in general that has allowed me to make such practical iterations with the work of others and in ways that have led to extensive consulting work over the years. Surely you, too, can become a window to scholarship and research in your chosen field or for an industry of intellectual interest to you, either nationally or regionally.

This brings an earlier point back to focus. Whatever type of consulting services you want to offer, there should be some industry concentration or focus. Without such focus, your scholarly hypotheses and research work will remain esoteric to your consulting market. Within this, learn which journals and periodicals are read by the executives of that industry and target your nontechnical publications there.

Speeches and Papers

As you become familiar with a particular industry, its problems, and how your work can be helpful to its executives, you also should discover which quarterly or annual conferences take place that are of great importance to your targeted industry. Just as your own academic society's regional and national conferences are sources of learning and new ideas for you, these conferences offer the same to specific areas of industry or business. Such conferences are scheduled and planned months, if not years, in advance. Often the location and dates will be set well before the conference even has a theme. By learning about these future get-togethers early in the process, through newspaper articles and industry newsletters, you can contact the conference organizers, offer a theme of interest to the industry, and get yourself on the speakers' list. Because most business people get tired of hearing from their own specialists year after year, conference after conference, if you are able to deliver a solid talk that provides practical new insights and advice to your audience, there is every reason to believe you will get additional offers to speak, not only at future industry conferences but also at key meetings held by industry leaders within their own companies. And through such notoriety, new clients can be developed on a fairly regular basis.

A different twist on speaking was provided by Delbecq of Santa Clara University. Delbecq recently talked about his methods of business development at a Gray Panthers seminar on managerial consultation at the Academy of Management. Delbecq's experience is that he only talks about what he knows and his research interests, but he notes that business executives find the presentation fascinating and are interested in how such ideas might be applied to their industry and company. Frequently, Delbecq has found himself doing action research within a company focused on his areas of interest, regardless of his lack of knowledge about the specific business or industry under scrutiny. It is by applying what he has learned in his field that he provides value-added service to his clients.

Tips for Public Speaking

As an aside, although there is not sufficient space in this book for a chapter on public speaking, I would share the following experience with you relative to talking to business executives on their own turf.

❶ Never plan to talk for more than 30 or 45 minutes. Whatever time remains of the slot you've been allotted, devote it to questions and answers with the audience.

❷ The smaller the audience (25-50), the better. Speeches delivered to rooms filled with hundreds of people in the audience are great for the ego but don't provide the intimacy needed for effective marketing of your ideas or your consulting practice.

❸ Always be sure to know who is in your audience. Are they human resource management specialists or financial executives and analysts or company presidents? Only through this knowledge can you tailor your remarks to address the concerns of the audience.

❹ No matter how much you want to say to your audience, pare it down to a few key information points that you believe your audience should understand, and stick to getting those three or four points across—no more or you risk losing your audience no matter how brilliant your presentation.

❺ Whether you have been given 30 minutes or 75, your talk should start by telling the audience what you are going to say, say it crisply and practically, and then close by telling your audience what you just said. This kind of forceful repetition is the basis of all marketing and advertising and assures that the mass of the audience will leave having understood what you wanted to communicate.

❻ Never talk as a scholar to a group of executives. Speak as an executives to other executives. Use the clinical "we" whenever possible. Your ability to identify with your audience is crucial to your credibility as an expert.

❼ Use visuals, preferably overhead transparencies, to make your key points or to demonstrate conclusions from your statistics, and have hard copies of those overheads available as handouts. Also, just in case the fifth estate is present, have at least two copies of your complete talk available as a handout.

❽ Contrary to popular myth, do not start or end your business speech with a joke to warm up your audience. They came to hear your expertise and insights, not your humor.

❾ Practice, practice, and practice. Start locally with a speech to the Southeastern Montana Association of Fortune 100 executives, for example, and keep at it. The more speaking you do, the better your opportunity to develop into an effective, dynamic speaker, sought out nationally by your audience.

❿ Always try to influence which speaking slot you will be assigned at conferences and conventions. Ideally, at some point in your career, you want to be the lead-off, keynote speaker. Failing this, try to get a slot on the morning programs, generally just before lunch. Failing this, try to be named the luncheon speaker. Whatever you do, avoid being scheduled to speak in the last hour of the last day of the conference. No one will come—trust me!

Interviews

As you publish more and more practical articles in popular periodicals, you may be approached by the media, either to contribute as an expert on a breaking story or as a source of real news based on the lay implications of your latest research. One way to ensure that this happens sooner rather than later is to let the media know you are an expert in your field or chosen industry. The most indirect method for doing this is the university public relations and press offices. Usually they provide lists of experts or public speakers to the media and interested audiences. If you are serious about developing a consulting practice, you should be on this list at your university before you finish reading this book!

When you are contacted by the media and the local television's panel truck parks outside your home or office, it can be very heady, and many inexperienced scholars lose their focus and abandon any strategy they might have had when contacting the media in the first place. There is an overwhelming urge to pontificate to the media. Don't do it. Remember your audience and talk as one of them. The most effective scientists on PBS programs, for example, are those that talk about their science and their hypotheses as if they were talking to "good ol' Harry," their next-door neighbor. And they do so in ways that communicate that they genuinely want you, the audience, to understand what it is that they have learned. To find more practical advice on dealing with the media, you should check out Fox and Levin (1993), which is another book in this series.

Op-Ed Letters

Another indirect marketing method is the op-ed letter to the local newspaper. If your perspective or expertise on a particular issue relates to current news issues, then you have every opportunity to have your views (as a local leading consultant and "spin doctor") published in the papers. But writing op-ed columns is very much akin to preparing industry-based speeches. You must keep it simple, short, and to the point and write in a style that addresses the newspaper's audience: your next-door neighbor, the man or woman down the street. Also, you should plan to write all this in no more than 500 words, and try for 400. If you are able to generate that kind of an article, then you should build a working relationship with one of the senior editors on the paper and offer articles on important subjects whenever you believe you have something to contribute as the local expert.

I developed such a working relationship with the business editor of the *Los Angeles Times* while teaching at the University of Southern California (USC). Frequently, he would call me for my opinion about issues in the financial services industry, and at least once a quarter he would ask me to do an article for him or participate in a series on a particular subject. When Bank of America was in serious financial and management troubles, he presented me as one of four experts on the bank and its problems. It was a stunning analysis by the paper. The layout of the article was very flattering with large individual pictures on the front page of the business section, something that could not be bought with $100,000 worth of public relations fees. Of course, I made numerous copies of the article, and because my picture was centered just under the *Los Angeles Times* masthead, I was able to use that piece for several years as a very credible marketing boost.

Writing a Monthly Column

Even without a background or training in journalism, your knowledge and understanding of your field and your chosen industry or issues, coupled with your ability to write succinctly, can lead to all manners of fame and fortune—to wit, a weekly, monthly, or quarterly column in the local newspaper or in an industry trade publication. In my own case, a series of op-ed articles on problems facing the banking industry led to an invitation from the editor of *Bankers Monthly* magazine to write a column on marketing strategy. This provided me with almost 10 years of a captive audience for my thoughts about banking strategy and marketing methods and led to endless consulting opportunities. However, writing scheduled columns is a bit like show business—the show must go on. As a result, if you commit to such a column, be it the monthly astronomy column in the local paper or something more down to earth in the *Insurance Underwriters Quarterly*, you must produce your column, and it must be usable for the editors every time. It is an enormous responsibility. If you are going on vacation, you need to write two or three columns in advance and submit them before you leave. Every column should be developed around topical issues and written for the journal's audience, not your scholarly peers.

I used my column as a window through which bankers could see into the world of business scholarship. I interpreted the latest statistical surveys or marketing theories for bankers to use in their day-to-day struggles with their competitors. Perhaps the need for such a resource was why the editors allowed me this privilege for so long. How could you develop a similar situation in your world?

Other Indirect Resources

There are a number of other sources of indirect marketing outlets for you and your work if you just look around you.

University and College Affiliations. Your university alumni association, especially that connected to your local business school, is a good source of contacts for your consulting efforts. Many successful alumni like to provide opportunities for faculty from their alma mater to contribute to their company. Also, local media executives can be met and nurtured through such channels.

Social Associations. The indirect marketing of consulting services has been around for a very long time. Just because you are an academic shouldn't prevent you from employing the same methods full-time consultants use, for example, joining the local country club or golf club, participating in the United Way and other local community charities, and finding other ways whereby you can get exposure to local major employers and industry and community leaders who may need your services someday if they only were aware of them.

Professional Associations. Once you have focused on a particular discipline or industry, there are any number of associations you should join to make contacts and begin networking so that people become aware of you and your consulting expertise. Such industry exposure also can lead to your inclusion on lists of organizations to contact whenever industry research is needed.

Being Your Own PR Department. As scholars and teachers, most of us tend to be a little shy as we experience the slings and arrows of our colleagues' questions and challenges every time we submit something for peer review and publication. It is a humbling experience. So we tend not to develop too much bravura. However, to build a lay image as an expert and to develop a successful consulting practice, you need a great deal of bravura. To paraphrase an old saw: Promoting yourself is a dirty job, but someone has to do it. If you don't, who will? So contact your university's Speakers' Bureau and the university's PR department; send a memo to your department head and dean informing them of your areas of interest and the fact that you are eager for consulting opportunities that can bring honor, respect, and research to your college, your department, and yourself.

Employing these and other indirect methods will, over the next 2 or 3 years, go a long way to putting you in the public eye and sensitizing the marketplace to the fact that you consult and are an available expert. But it is interesting to see that we are ending on a note about bravura. *Bravura* is a good word to use to connect indirect marketing efforts with direct marketing efforts.

3 | Direct Marketing Strategies

Having worked hard to try out some of the suggestions offered in the area of indirect marketing, you probably do not yet have a client. You're still not a consultant. When all else fails, it is time to perform direct marketing.

What Is Direct Marketing?

Direct marketing is your own, proactive sales effort to attract, capture, and hold consulting clients, individuals, and companies. Direct marketing consists of anything from "cold"-calling prospects on the telephone to contacting private enterprises and government agencies to have your name put on the list of consultants authorized to receive requests for proposals (RFPs) on a routine basis. Direct marketing methods also entail your developing or synthesizing industry or topical issues of current interest to business executives and designing a mail campaign to get appointments with them. It could even consist of ads placed in industry journals for copies of your latest research. Anything you do directly and overtly to capture clients is considered direct marketing.

As mentioned in the previous chapter, for decades, direct marketing efforts were snubbed by prestige consulting firms as beneath them—unprofessional—and certainly unnecessary. Conversely, smaller firms not worried about their general image and most independent consultants had to use direct marketing efforts just for the basic recognition of their niche in the marketplace.

However, beginning in the mid-1980s, the consulting profession changed dramatically. With a surfeit of knowledge-based practices, an overabundance of corporate executives forced into early retirement in many industries, and the slowing of the economy generally, a number of premiere consulting firms that had never resorted to direct marketing tactics before, began aggressive mailing and marketing campaigns, and in some cases actually sent people out, door-to-door, to shake new clients from the trees. Some of these efforts, as in the case of Andersen Consulting, were composed of slick and effective advertisements in leading newspapers and business journals. Other efforts were a disaster and did little to enhance the reputation of the profession. The continued decline of the U.S. economy in the late 1980s and early 1990s placed even greater pressure on the profession. One of the areas hardest hit was executive education and management training. As the economy worsened, more and more corporations slashed their training budgets along with advertising and outside consulting costs. Old-line firms—such as Harbridge House, which for decades was a leader in executive development—were forced to start laying off professional staff.

Direct marketing efforts have become de rigueur for any firm that wants to protect existing clientele and expand. Today, no one thinks badly of any effort taken with good taste and ethics that is aimed at developing clientele, be it for an existing firm or a novice scholar. In fact, it is about the only way to generate meaningful consulting business as we approach a new century. This chapter looks at how you can take control of your fledgling consulting practice and develop clients in 90 days or less.

Developing Consulting Alliances

The simplest direct approach for a scholar, especially one in the business field, is to identify a local area consulting firm interested in having a scholar's insights and research available for its clientele and to develop a working relationship with that firm. A classic example of such a relationship, perhaps one of several hundred in the profession today, is that of Warren MacFarland, one of the leading information systems faculty at the Harvard Business School, and his ongoing relationship with the INDEX Group, a knowledge boutique serving the information systems marketplace globally. MacFarland became associated with the INDEX Group some years ago because it could provide him the full-time consulting staff he required to perform certain kinds of research and to staff larger information system projects internationally. With MacFarland as an associate, the INDEX Group was able to see immeasurable new business, while MacFarland has the opportunity to design and conduct seminal information systems research on the cutting edge of global business issues. It is a symbiotic relationship, and thus it comes as no surprise that about the time MacFarland became chair of the Harvard Business School's information systems department, he also was invited to join the board of directors of the INDEX Group.

Although few of us are as brilliant as MacFarland, and fewer consulting firms are as professional or have developed the sophisticated international clientele the INDEX Group has, such firm-scholar strategic and marketing alliances are becoming more and more typical of the industry today. As a matter of fact, few knowledge boutiques can exist without a relationship with one or more leading scholars in a particular discipline or industry. We are their principal source of new ideas, theories, and seminal research. And such trends tend to feed on themselves as sophisticated clients are now more apt to ask a consulting firm who their resident scholars are and with which business schools they are affiliated.

Scholar affiliations with professional consulting firms have every potential to be as dynamic and as successful as the example given above. Scholars need opportunities to research current and emerging issues of interest in their fields and in society in general. Consulting firms have clients with very complex problems and issues, especially because competition in global markets continues to intensify. The consulting firm can deliver the client and provide staff and administrative support for large projects, the scholar can deliver the research and the insights. Together they can provide the client with real competitive advantage and an ephemeral edge in their markets. The scholar gets to publish his or her research, which, because it is on a hot topic or an emerging global issue, stands a better chance of publication in a leading journal, and that article, in turn, can lead to more business.

The key for a scholar is, first and foremost, to find a reputable firm with a clientele of interest to him or her and a clientele that places value and importance on the research and focus of the scholar. That is the hard part. And it is particularly hard for scholars working and living outside major metropolitan areas, where most knowledge-based firms are located. If you are connected with a college or university in a rural area, you may have to extend your search regionally to find the right consulting organization.

If and when you are able to do so, then the issues remaining are to scope out the relationship. What are you willing to do for the firm, what is the firm willing to do for you? Can they live with your teaching schedule and your publication deadlines? Can you live with their fee structure and some form of minimum monthly guarantee?

Developing Direct Sales Campaigns

Should you be unable to find the right consulting firm or should you simply decide to go it alone, a proven but more aggressive direct marketing approach is driven off letter campaigns that you can design and execute. The classic letter campaign works as follows:

Select an Industry. Preferably, you will choose an industry that you have some interest in and insights about. Even if you can't come up with a specific industry, identify one that is in the news and apparently troubled. Perform some library research to determine the three or four key issues that probably are putting enormous pressure on any chief executive serving in that industry. Examples really are easy:

Banking. What must be done to develop and maintain a balanced lending portfolio, one that will not yield overconcentrations in construction lending every 7 years, forcing a merger?

Health care. What can be done to reduce administrative systems costs while still maintaining the controls needed to ensure that the client is not robbed blind? What will be the impact of government regulation and price/fee controls?

Aerospace. What technologies and processes does the firm possess that can lead to new, useful, and successful consumer products to replace the billions in lost Pentagon business?

Insurance. What are the products and services that will attract the younger, more sophisticated customers of the 21st century, customers more concerned about increased cash flow than saving for the future?

A list of three or four such issues for your selected industry should not be difficult to develop. These issues can then be confirmed in conversations with local executives in that industry under the guise of research.

Develop a Mailing List. Create a mailing list of the companies in your selected industry. Begin your list with those firms nearby and work outward from your home base in concentric geographic circles. In this way, as you contact interested companies, travel costs can be controlled. In developing your list of prospective companies, always try to obtain the name of the president, CEO, or chairman. This is the individual to whom you want your letter directed. Company presidents have more authority and access to the checkbook, which are required to hire consultants, than any other executive in the organization. They do not necessarily have to go through a marketing committee or an operations group, and even if they refer you to other executives, that referral is from the president!

Develop an Issues Letter. With your list of company CEOs and their addresses, you now need to develop a brief letter. The purpose of the letter is only to catch the executive's attention. This is done by demonstrating that you know and understand something of their issues, problems, and pressures. You want to give the impression that you are someone worth meeting, if only for a chat. As a scholar, perhaps you have some answers to difficult issues. Figure 3.1 presents a copy of such a letter. Select an industry with which you have some familiarity and try to develop a similar letter.

Mail 10 Letters a Week. Executives are very busy people. Most work 12 hours a day; some, 7 days a week. Therefore, you will have to follow up each letter with as many as a half dozen telephone calls to get through. They are out of town. They are traveling. They are in meetings. They are on vacation. The point being, that if you send out more than 10 letters each week, on average, you will have more than 60 phone calls to place the following week. It is better to go slowly mailing only 10 letters weekly rather than have someone on your list receive a letter that states you will be calling shortly only to have your call come in 1 or 2 months. By then the recipient has forgotten the letter. Keep in mind that just as the letter was merely to get their attention, so, too, the phone call is only to arrange a meeting. You still haven't begun to sell your services or anything else to this point. You would never want to sell anything as sophisticated as consulting services over the tele-

April 1, 1993

Mr. John Usurious
President and CEO
Last Bank of Cleveland
23 Disintermediation Boulevard
Cleveland, OH 33345

Dear Mr. Usurious:

These are particularly challenging times for U.S. business executives, perhaps no more so than in the banking industry. CEOs are faced with

- Fewer and fewer exclusive, profitable products to offer
- More and more nonbank competition in traditional commercial and retail markets
- Increased competition from foreign banks that often have sources of inexpensive funds
- Increasingly high operating expenses
- Ever greater nonperforming segments of the loan portfolio as a result of the weakened economy.

I believe I have some new ideas and approaches to address these issues based on research I performed recently at State School of Road and Mines. I would like to meet and talk with you about these issues at your convenience. To that end, I will call you in the next few days.

Sincerely yours,

Harry Hoot
Professor of Antiquated Industries

Figure 3.1. A Sample Issues Letter

phone in any event. It is too easy for the party on the other end of the line just to hang up, severing the tenuous relationship.

Follow Up With Phone Calls. Again, the purpose of the phone call is to get an appointment with the executive. One of the most difficult exercises often is getting past the president's secretary or administrative assistant. Staff personnel tend to be highly protective of their bosses and frequently try to handle less important issues on their superiors' behalf. As a result, you will be facing a barrage of questions such as: "Does Mr. Usurious know you?" (I certainly haven't heard your name around the board room!), "Will Ms. Paperweight know what this is about?" (What are you trying to sell us, anyway?), and "I don't recall seeing your letter, let me pass your call down to Mr. Hyperbole in personnel. Perhaps he can help you" (If you're looking for a job, forget it!).

In most instances, these are legitimate questions, if for no other reason than that the executive probably insists on knowing who's on the phone before he or she takes a call. The secretary would like to be able to say something like, "Mr. Usurious, there's a Professor Hoot on the phone. He [or she] says he [or she] sent you a letter last week about some critical industry issues. He [or she] would like to visit with you." All this means is that you need not personalize the protective efforts of the secretary. Tell the truth, be factual, and be very, very pleasant. Also be persistent. You may have to call Mr. Usurious's office a dozen times before you catch him in, free, and willing to take your call. And all the time you are going to have to deal with his secretary, Bruce, or his MBA administrative assistant, Muffy. You need these people's help to get through. Be nice!

If you are unable to get through after weeks of trying, you have nothing to lose by trying a very aggressive strategy. Fax a copy of your original letter and pencil a note at the bottom: "Have been trying to call you for two weeks now and am unable to get through." Call again the next day. Don't use your doctoral title in these calls—you might be mistaken for a medical doctor and completely confuse the situation ("There's a Dr. Strangelove on the line. He [or she] says your tests have come back from the lab!").

Conduct Sales Calls. Having sent out your letters, and made dozens of phone calls, you will find that for each 10 letters, on average, you are getting one appointment. This is a typical sales experience. Selling, of any kind, is a *statistical* exercise. So many letters equate to so many appointments. So many meetings equate to so many requests for proposals, and so many proposals will equate, over time, to work. But it is important for you to realize that if you are persistent, *you will generate business* using this approach. My own records show that when I started a full-time consulting practice a few years ago, my partner and I sent out 110 letters, followed by 680 phone calls. They generated only 28 appointments. Of these, 7 prospects canceled on us and 21 meetings took place. The meetings resulted in 15 proposals that led to three major contracts generating more than $350,000 for the partnership, or $175,000 each. This works out statistically to a value of more than $235 per original phone call. If I offered you $235 for every phone call you made this afternoon, how many would you be willing to make? I know this reads like one of those business books, *How I Sold $10 million in Life Insurance in 10 Weeks,* but this is what marketing is about, whether you are selling shoes, brushes, insurance, or sophisticated scientific knowledge. You are in a numbers game!

Sample Letters

Take another look at Figure 3.1, which is a sample of the kind of issues letter you will want to develop. If possible, you should try to put all your thoughts on one page and make them concise. Remember, the only purpose of the letter is to get the attention of your prospect. *You are not trying to sell anything with this letter,* only demonstrating your understanding of the industry issues facing an executive in that industry.

The sample letter is geared to motivate recipients to accept your call and meet with you. However, some academics are concerned that if they haven't focused on a particular industry and its issues for 10 or more years, they shouldn't posture themselves as an industry expert. Expertise is relative. Most executives do not reserve time in their busy schedules to read much beyond the news periodicals. They rely on their staff to read the deeper journals and research articles and attend conferences. This, however, leaves them captives of their own hectic schedules with little time for reflection. To meet with an academic, even a graduate student, who has spent 1 or 2 years focused impartially on an industry or its issues can be refreshing for a harried executive. It really doesn't take 10 years to develop a perspective that is valuable to an industry executive.

On the other hand, if the tone and style of the sample letter in Figure 3.1 is too strong for you, Figure 3.2 presents what I would label an announcement letter. This letter is modeled on one my colleagues and I recently sent to more than 600 attorneys. The thrust of the letter merely informs the recipient that there is a new organization, a new consultant, a new practice in the neighborhood should he or she have knowledge of a prospect who might be aided by such expertise. Actually, it leans toward an indirect sales approach, but it, too, can be used as a basis for face-to-face meetings.

Managing Interviews

Let's say that you used the more aggressive issues letter, the indirect announcement letter, or even one of your own design; sent out hundreds of letters; and followed up with phone calls. You have now generated some meetings for yourself. Congratulations! Now what? The hard part in all this marketing effort is rapidly approaching. You are going to have to structure and manage an interview, the purpose of which is not to sell the prospect anything, but to provide the prospect with an opportunity to share his or her problems with you. In turn, your goal is to surface and identify what really is troubling the prospect. It is hoped that the problem will be something you are in a position to help with based on your experience and unique knowledge. However, if you are an expert in the financial services industry and the bank president tells you his or her real problem is being rejected

April 1, 1993

Susan Dewey, Esquire
Managing Partner
Dewey, Cheetum, & Howe
Attorneys-at-Law
3 Court Street
Malfeasance, MN 99766

Dear Susan:

Recently, I established a consulting practice to share my ten years of experience in studying the issues leading to troubled businesses and counseling small-business owners. My primary objective is to help distressed businesses avoid severe financial loss or even bankruptcy, quickly stabilizing their situations by providing hands-on, interim management services, often as acting chief executive or chief financial officer. The strength of my practice is the breadth and depth of experience associated with years of research and personal experience in crisis management in over a dozen industries. There are several key situations in which my services are apt to be most useful:

> Financially distressed companies for which profitability or cash flow difficulties have led to problems with the IRS, trade creditors, and financial institutions.
>
> Family-owned and -managed businesses in which relationships are interfering with the success of the business—divorce, sibling rivalry, and/or generational differences; objective interim management must be provided while such issues are resolved or the business is sold.
>
> Partnership disputes that require independent management until the issues can be resolved.
>
> Death or incapacity of the owner/manager when there is no one able to maintain interim leadership.

Should you learn of or encounter any such situations where my services may be of help, please call. All consultations are strictly confidential and the initial consultation is free of charge or obligation.

Sincerely,

Dudley Dewrite, Ph.D.
Assistant Professor, Finance
School of Accounting

Figure 3.2. A Sample Announcement Letter

by his or her 49-year-old son who refuses to become the next bank president; or you are a health care expert, but learn the real problem at the hospital is labor-management issues; or you are a specialist in pre-Columbian art objects, but find the problem at the museum is an antiquated accounting system, then you should refer the prospect to someone with the expertise they need.

Marketing professional services is truly an act of self-discipline, the same self-discipline you employed to get yourself through the writing of your dissertation. Marketing and sales require courageous efforts, but they can and do pay off.

Returning to your marketing campaign and the impending interview, the best method and approach is to role-play the part of your prospect. What is he or she thinking about you and what actions is he or she assuming you will take? Your host probably remembers that you sent a letter about industry issues. He or she may assume that you are there to try to sell something and is seeing you, more often than not, out of curiosity and the opportunity to spend time with someone who has a different perspective on the business. All well and good.

In fact, you are entering the meeting without the slightest idea what the contact's problems are. And, the worst thing you can do is guess what they might be, only to spend a half hour trying to sell something he or she doesn't need or want. What to do? The secret is to *ask!* A method I have used successfully for more than 20 years is a simple trilogy of questions:

1. What's going well for you and your business? Where and why are you successful? What are you doing right?

2. What's not going well for the business? Where and why are you having problems or disappointments?

3. What are your dreams? What special projects and new ideas have you had for some time, but because of a lack of money, people, or time, they just never seem to get top priority?

Obviously you cannot just walk into a room with a stranger to ask about his or her deepest fears. You need to establish some level of trust first. One way to do that is to make the contact feel comfortable, not threatened. Begin by allowing the contact to feel that his or her assumptions were correct— take a few minutes to introduce yourself and to talk a little about your work and research *as it applies to the contact's business and in lay terms.* Do not act professorial or in any way pontificate. If you do, the relationship will be still-born. The old saw that you never get a second chance to make a first impression is never more true than in these kinds of meetings. Prospects want to meet a professional equal, someone they can share problems with and not someone who is superior, someone who is going to tell them how to run the business, or someone who may think badly of them because they do not have graduate degrees.

After no more than 5 minutes of talking about yourself and your work, give the prospect a chance to loosen up, to brag a little about his or her successes, and to relate the things that make him or her feel good. By talking about something they can feel good about, people tend to relax. Your job at this point is to listen, and then listen some more. You might wedge in a follow-up question such as, "How long have you had this strategy?" or "When did you realize you had a success?" But allow the prospect to carry on for a while.

It is usually possible to make a smooth transition from good news to bad news, and you will find a natural pause in the conversation to ask the prospect just that. If you have communicated some warmth, a little humanity, sincerity, and a nonthreatening posture to the prospect up to this point, he or she will tell you. Listen! Listen carefully and ask questions to allow as much information to surface as you need to understand the issue, its history, and what has been done to date to resolve it.

Finally, allow the prospect a chance to tell his or her ideas and hopes. Get the prospect talking about pet projects, research he or she would like to perform, or training he or she would like to install in the organization.

Human nature is a fascinating thing. I cannot explain why this approach works, but I have been advising colleagues to try it for many years. Invariably, I get calls telling me how incredulous they were upon using it. A typical reaction is, "I couldn't believe it! After just 10 minutes, they told me all their problems—me, a total stranger, a lowly doctoral candidate! I never would have thought I could do it!"

There are some other important questions to employ during this discussion. Critical data must surface if you are to position yourself to sell some consulting or training or research work. These questions include:

- Who else feels this is a problem (who are your allies in the organization)?
- Does everyone feel this way (who doesn't agree with you and why)?
- What have you tried to date to resolve this issue (what hasn't worked so far and why)?
- Have you ever used consultants here—for anything (do you know how consultants work and what they cost; what expectations do you have in working with me)?
- Have you discussed this particular issue with other consultants (do I have a clean shot at this or am I up against competition, and if so, who)?
- Do you have a budget to address this problem (have you set aside funds or will this become a financial cause célèbre in the organization if you try to hire me)?

Finally, there are two more questions to ask, which many consultants believe are the most difficult ones. This is where *you ask for the business.* If you never do, you'll never have a client, but for some reason, many potential consultants get cold feet a this point. It probably has a lot to do with setting yourself up for rejection, but you cannot personalize this kind of rejection. It is a statistical phenomenon that you will be rejected four out of five times initially, and one out of two times as you become more experienced at selling professional services. It has nothing to do with you, so don't worry about it. These two final questions are:

- May I develop and send you a proposal to work with you on this problem?
- What would be the process for such a proposal to be approved?

The first of these queries identifies if your conversation has been successful. Have you created credibility and trust? Does the prospect sincerely want help with the issues discussed? Do you have a chance to be that instrument of change? The second question is equally vital. It tells you who else is to be involved in the decision-making process, pointing you in the direction you need to go to get the business. There will be others in the organization you will have to talk with and win over. As more and more companies empower their employees, many such decisions, especially about bringing in outsiders, become team decisions. Furthermore, if there is a committee or task force involved in the decision making, you will want to be present and available to answer questions about your proposal and your work when that group meets to discuss your proposal. *Never allow the prospect or any other third party to try to sell your services for you.* Other people cannot answer questions about you or your capabilities. That is something only you can do directly.

Tables 3.1 and 3.2 present questions that you should review before you go into one of these meetings. You should use these lists a basis for setting the scene for proposal development. More and more, your initial written proposal will be only a prelude to your appearance before a group of managers and employees who will play some part in the final decision

Table 3.1 Twenty Questions to Ask a Prospect (an Interview Checklist)

1. What kind of project do you have in mind?
2. Why are you considering this project?
3. What might be the ultimate objective?
4. What are your overall concerns regarding this project?
5. What is the general range of needs on the project?
6. What do you believe is needed to solve the problem?
7. Whose idea was the project originally?
8. Any specific solutions you know of?
9. Who developed the project? Who is its sponsor?
10. Who is supportive of the work? Who is opposed to it? Why?
11. What is the source of the funding? Is there a formal budget?
12. Has your organization ever used consultants before?
13. Have other consultants been contacted about this project?
14. Have any commitments been made? Project criteria established?
15. What are the most important attributes for the consultants to have?
16. To whom are the consultants to be accountable? Is there a time frame?
17. How did you get involved in the project?
18. How will the success or failure of the project affect you?
19. What is your role now? What will it be?
20. Who will decide who gets this contract?

to hire you. You should not be put off by such protocol. If you are to be a successful consultant, you will need the support of a number of people within the client's organization, and it will be your sales ability with them as well as your charm and professionalism with the CEO that will lock you into the job.

When you come out of your initial interview, remember that you actually have three opportunities: to support an already successful strategy or program, to address a pressing problem, and to help realize a project no one else has had the time to do. In the next chapter we will discuss the development of your proposal and how to deliver a dynamic oral presentation to capture a client.

Table 3.2 Ten Questions to Ask Yourself

---

1. Have I had enough time with the prospect to understand the issues?
2. Is the prospect serious about hiring an outside consultant, and did I really surface why they might be interested in a scholar such as myself?
3. Have I identified who the real client is? Is there more than one client here? If so, do I understand their needs?
4. Does the client know how to use consultants effectively?
5. Can I really perform this work and is there a valuable role I can play for the company? Do I have enough information, reports, statistics, and minutes of meetings to develop a coherent proposal?
6. Am I proposing the best project to address the issues? Is this work that has priority for the client?
7. Am I dealing with the person who can authorize this work? If not, how can I talk to him or her?
8. Is there a high probability for the success of this project, and did I cover the potential risks with the prospect in our discussions?
9. Do I have agreement from the prospect on the budget, my fees and expenses, the time frame for the work to be done, and the level of support they will provide me?
10. Is this really a good project to pursue and spend time on, or are there other consultants involved who are more capable or better positioned to get the job?

---

4 | "Sales" Is Not a Four-Letter Word

To this point in the marketing process, having used both direct and indirect methods, you placed yourself in front of a prospective client and have been asked to submit a proposal. And in spite of everything you think you have done to this point, the selling of the work has just begun. From this point forward you must successfully:

→ Sell the client what he or she wants—later you can sell what he or she needs.
→ Sell the client on the way you will work.
→ Sell the client on the end result of your work—the benefits.
→ Sell the client on working with you in partnership.
→ Sell the client on performing part of the work himself or herself to free your time for analytical efforts.
→ Sell the client on your findings and conclusions.
→ Sell the client on the best solution.
→ Sell more work.

For You, Today, We Got a Special!

In between all this selling, you might actually get to perform some brilliant consulting work. Why does the thought of selling bother so many academics so profoundly? Most of us grow up hearing our parents and peers talking negatively about salespeople they had met, ones who aggravated and annoyed them. We all can recall salespeople who thoroughly distressed us: They were rude, insensitive, self-oriented, and generally ill-mannered. And, certainly, we didn't go through all our own scholarly pain and suffering to end up as sales-people, no better than a used-car merchant or a hawker of Oriental steak knives on late-night television!

Fair enough. Unfortunately, so much of our academic work is based on solid research and robust statistical findings that many conclusions appear self-evident, so we think that there shouldn't be any need to sell anything. Right? Wrong! You have to sell the hypothesis to get the research grant. You have to sell the subject on allowing you to do the research with him or her. You have to sell everyone involved on the notion that this is an important research project. And once you have completed your work, you have to sell your conclusions to your peers. You sell your article to an editor and a review board. It goes on and on. As scholars, there well may be as much selling and salescraft connected with our chosen career than any other, even direct sales of tangible products. Larry Greiner of the University of Southern California, a renowned consulting scholar, talks of the value of heuristic experience. He points out that we constantly rely on our experience yet seldom acknowledge its importance. For scholars, this is particularly true with respect to the subjects of sales and selling. Often, scholars deny their sales abilities and denigrate themselves for being highly ineffective marketers.

You sold yourself to obtain your current position. You may be actively involved in selling yourself again to obtain a better position. What, then, is the psychological hangup among academics about proactively selling themselves as consult-ants? The answer appears to rest with how that effort is per-formed. It is an issue of *style.* All of us can recall at least one absolutely obnoxious salesperson. On reflection, that person left a permanent scar on our image of salespeople. Probably he or she was rude and called us at a very inconvenient time to talk about what was important to him or her. The salesperson addressed us by our first name, assuming a familiarity that did not exist. He or she would not listen to our needs or our objections, but continued to push the product on us even when it was not what we wanted. That salesperson promised us things that were not true. All of these aspects of a detested sales style are real. What it should teach us is that putting *your* needs before those of your prospect will generate bad feelings.

Conversely, each of us can think back to a salesperson we met who impressed us positively: He or she was polite; sensitive; and sincerely curious about our needs, our specifications, and our ability to pay. He or she asked us questions, listened to our answers, and was patient. This salesperson worked with us on our schedule not his or hers. I could go on and on. The point is that there is a professional way to sell your ideas and products and there is an unprofessional way. It should come as no surprise, then, to learn that the most successful professional consultants are not always the most technically competent or the most scholarly. Rather they are the ones who come across to prospects as the most understanding, the most concerned, the most willing to help. This is not to infer that they are not technically competent or cerebral in their work. It should teach us that personal marketing style is as important as content and craft!

Developing the Work Plan

The first step to preparing a proposal is to prepare a detailed work plan of the project. What exactly are you proposing to do? Research? If so, are the data available or will you need time to develop new data or even a new reporting system for the client's company? Is all this going to take 1 or 2 days or weeks of your time? Is there anyone within the client's firm who can help you perform this work, freeing your time and your budget for other things? Where will you be performing this data development: in your office at the university or on-site at the client's factory in another location?

Will you have to design a questionnaire or a computer program to process the results? How many hours or days will it take? Who can help you with the data review: a graduate student, a colleague, someone else? What should he or she be paid?

What are the client's expectations for a final product? Does he or she want a hefty 300-page report or an oral presentation before the executive committee? If a report is needed, how long will it take you to create? Can someone else do the writing, the graphics, the art work, or the financial analyses?

In planning and designing your project, you must be certain you have allowed sufficient time for the human side of the project, too: interaction with the client's employees and committees, subcontractors, or suppliers; leeway for delays and contingencies; time for preparation and presentation of progress reports; and allowance for additional research and data development to support the findings as they surface.

All of this should culminate in a detailed listing of your time (full and partial days), the time of any colleagues, staff, students, or researchers you intend to involve, and the expenses that may result from the project (e.g., travel and supplies). Finally, before using this work plan as a foundation for your proposal, review it one last time to ensure that you really need all the time you have projected. Can you do the work in a few days less? Do you really need the help you have built in? What is the bare-bones cost for the client to get the work done?

Developing the Proposal

Once a prospect has communicated sincere interest in working with you and you have reviewed your checklists (Tables 3.1 and 3.2) and detailed your work plan, you must develop a written proposal. This is the first formal step toward closing the sale. Here are six reasons for this:

❶ *It provides an opportunity to test the issues.* You had a very exciting and encouraging hour with the prospects. They shared some real problems with you and were impressed with your perspectives and your field work last summer. They asked you to submit a proposal. This is a pregnant moment, because if you propose to do something that seems perfectly logical to you but that the prospects believe does not address the issues, you will never get the work. A written proposal allows you the chance to restate the issues and what ought to be done about them. If there is a misunderstanding, this allows you the opportunity to surface that misunderstanding and to clarify the issues. It is better to be discussing the issues a second time than to be rejected out of hand.

❷ *It allows you to think through your approach.* Having put your understanding of the issues down in writing as clearly and tersely as possible, you now have the opportunity to think through what exactly you are proposing to do for the prospect. Will you perform seminal research or just interpret existing data? Will you develop your data locally, regionally, or nationally? Will you do all the work yourself? Will you present your findings to the marketing committee or the board of directors? Will your final report consist of an oral presentation or a 200-page report? These are fundamental points for you to think through and for the prospects to understand.

❸ *It allows you to explain your methodology.* When will you start? How long will the project take? Will you do it entirely on your own or will you have colleagues or graduate students helping? Will you expect the clients to provide staff? Will there be interim reports on your progress? What resources will you need from the client? What will be the end result or product? How will it resolve the clients' problem or meet their needs? By committing your process and thinking to paper in a detailed work plan, you demonstrate to the clients that you are a professional. It allows the clients to understand your thought process and work style. It gives you the chance to clarify what needs to be done and what you will require.

❹ *It clarifies the relationship.* By writing down who will be doing what, the time frame for each stage of the work, and the resources you will provide or expect from the client, the working relationship for the project is established. Again, it provides the clients with the opportunity to say, "Well, that's not exactly what we had in mind" or "We agree with you, but let's include George" or "This is fine, but for that stage of the work you should report to Caroline in research."

❺ *It establishes your compensation and costs.* This is your opportunity to review thoroughly your work plan assumptions. How many days, performing what kinds of work? What will you have to pay your assistants or subcontractors? How much travel is involved and what will that cost? What kind of materials and supplies will you need to develop and deliver the training materials promised or any other hard product? A very important part of this step in the formal proposal is to think through whether or not the clients can afford such fees. Is it what they expected and budgeted for? Or might too large a number implode the entire opportunity?

❻ *It allows you to sell the benefits of the work.* Just as we discussed in the brief section about speech making, proposals are basic communication vehicles whereby you tell the client what you are going to do, how you are going to do it, and the benefits that your work will provide. This is the closing moment of your sales effort. What does the client really want: consensus among the senior managers, a plan or a planning process, and/or new opportunities or methods to exploit existing opportunities? Put more succinctly: Just what is the client getting for his or her money?

Figure 4.1 presents an example of a proposal letter. Note there are six parts to the letter, one corresponding to each of the six points made above. If any one is omitted from a proposal, even from the most casual type of proposal (an oral agreement and a handshake), then there is an opportunity for confusion and misunderstanding to take the upper hand. Developing and refining proposals professionally is a major part of a successful consultant's discipline. Table 4.1 is a proposal review form that you can use as a checklist to ensure that your proposal is as professional as it can be.

Types of Proposals

There is no end to the style and method of proposals. The most casual, and the one with the highest risk of misunderstanding, is the oral agreement and the traditional handshake. Usually, this level of proposal is among colleagues, peers, or friends or with existing, satisfied clients eager to buy additional work. But in the heat of conflict and crisis, who can remember what was agreed on 3 months previously when there was still inventory and the chief financial officer hadn't run off to Brazil with the bookkeeper? One of the worst things imaginable is to get crossed with a client over your fees and the costs involved with a project. Another distressing situation is when the client expects more than what you recall promising or something you didn't even consider. A third area for serious disagreement is the scheduling of the work. It gets particularly sticky when the client has been delaying and deferring all along, but when the project is 3 months behind schedule, the client says it's your fault.

All of these situations occur frequently when nothing is committed to writing. And any of these totally unnecessary misunderstandings can unfairly tarnish your reputation as a consultant or even as a scholar. Certainly, any one of them will ensure that you do not get repeat business from that client.

Proposals can range from a handshake to bound volumes. Most of the work proposed by individuals managing a solo practice can be stated and summarized in a simple letter. This is the most straightforward kind of proposal, one that does not require anything on the part of the client but a verbal agreement as to when you can start. Fully 95% of all my consulting work over the past 2 decades resulted from such letters, most of them no more than three or four pages long.

The next level of formality in proposals is to ask the client to sign an enclosed copy of the proposal letter and return it to you, formally contracting with you to perform the work. Even more formal is a request that the signed copy be returned to you accompanied with a check for some amount of down payment to cover materials, startup costs on large complex projects, material for training programs, and so on. For example, if you are performing an organizational attitudinal survey and the survey questionnaire costs $50 to reproduce, and

Table 4.1 Proposal Review Form

Proposal Segment	Minimal Acceptable Effort	Professional- Quality Proposal
Understanding of the issues	Nature, basis, and history of the problem explained	Discusses causes and effects, covers broader implications of key facts
The proposal	Explains purpose of the proposal and how it will resolve the issues and describes final product	Includes impact of the project on other areas and discusses results the work will achieve
The methodology	Details the work to be done and skills needed; includes work plan narrative	Work plan may be added graphically together with critical path diagram; focus on inter-task relationships
Timing and responsibility	Clearly scoped schedules and anticipated client support and reporting relationships	Discusses possible limitations of the work and provides alternatives to overcome limitations
Fee estimates	Provides dollar total or range of fees and notes expenses separately; states timing of payments	Relates fees to project phases, shows careful justification of expenses; may include alternate payment schedules in consideration of impact on client cash flows
Benefits	Lists significant benefits to be gained from the work; describes intangible benefits to be had	Discusses timing of benefits to be had; links benefits to client actions following the project; diagrams what is versus what can be

the client asks that 200 employees receive the questionnaire, you would be out-of-pocket $10,000. You should ask for this amount up front.

When working with government agencies, public utilities, or any organization open to public scrutiny, you will find the

(*text continued on page 61*)

May 21, 1993

Mr. Wendell Widget
President and CEO
Worldwide Widgets, Inc.
333 Widget Boulevard
Wendell, OH 77665

Dear Wendell:

The generosity of your time and that of everyone I met at Worldwide Widgets was extraordinary. My sincerest thanks. This letter is to set out how I propose to assist you in introducing a formal total quality management (TQM) program to the company.

MY UNDERSTANDING OF THE ISSUES

It is my understanding that Worldwide Widgets is at a crucial growth point in its historical development. New orders for larger and larger widgets are coming in whereby the company will double in size in the next 18 to 20 months. Furthermore, market opportunities abound both domestically and overseas such that the company's sales may double again to as much as $500 million by 1998, in spite of a relatively conservative marketing strategy.

A major force behind this growth is the distinctive competence of Worldwide Widgets as a "service" factory, providing field consultation on difficult problems to client organizations, coupled with the firm's "can-do" delivery policy on standard widget products.

For the company to absorb this projected growth whereby it protects and maintains its distinctive competence and its reputation for quality, and to help position the enterprise for even greater growth beyond the year 2000, the owners and senior management would like to introduce TQM principles in the firm so that the company can strengthen and intensify its commitment to excellence and quality, regardless of the scale of its operations.

At the same time, the owners and senior management recognize that TQM is not a temporary management fad but rather a fundamental change in the way work is planned, designed, and performed in all areas of the company from the production floor to the accounting department. Furthermore, the quest for TQM is not a trip with a midpoint and an end, but an unending, permanent process of continuous improvement. In other words, it is a way of life.

As a result, it will be the commitment of the owners and managers of the firm to accept responsibility for developing and managing such a program, and it is their responsibility to enroll all employees over time. Based on the

Figure 4.1. Sample Proposal Letter

criticality of this mission, it is not something that can be delegated on a surrogate basis to outside consultants or productivity experts.

THE PROPOSAL

Based on our discussions on May 5, I propose to work with the owners and senior management to develop and help execute a TQM program for World-wide Widgets in three stages.

Stage 1. Within the next 90 days, I will custom design and deliver an intense 2-day program to introduce TQM and its principles to the top 20 managers of the firm.

Stage 2. Within the next 180 days, work will begin with each of the department heads across the organization to support their efforts at determining the specific roles and objectives of the departments in a TQM effort. Furthermore, the department heads will be encouraged to design and implement a series of specific projects that incorporate TQM processes in their areas of responsibility. Much of this Stage 2 activity will comprise TQM training for all employees and assistance to the department heads in enrolling employees in the process whereby they accept ownership of TQM principles without feeling threatened by the changes in their work or their job design.

In addition, at the outset, to ensure the ongoing success of the overall effort and specific projects, an executive steering committee should be formed from senior managers to guide the overall TQM effort; an issues management team must be formed of senior and middle managers to work on key issues of operating policies as they are affected by TQM processes, and unit management teams need to be formed by senior and middle managers to guide and support quality progress in their units and across specific departmental lines. The success of any TQM effort relies heavily on the involvement and effectiveness of these working teams during the 1st or 2nd year of the TQM effort.

Stage 3. Beginning in the first quarter of next year, work will commence with the department heads to merge their collective TQM projects and experiments into an overall and interlocking TQM process across the firm, whereby TQM drives all processes, from providing employees with statistical information to constructing valves on the shop floor to shipping, receiving, accounting, engineering, research and development, and so on.

Furthermore, as the TQM process becomes fully integrated, improvement teams composed of various individuals, including customers, vendors, and distributors, are formed to conduct improvement projects on inbound and outbound and service systems; and self-managed work groups composed of employees and section leaders are formed to manage and improve specific processes. (Some of these may be formed earlier in Stage 2 efforts.)

Figure 4.1. Continued

Although Murphy's Law still can and does rule in TQM process schedules, within 18 months, and parallel to the firm's projected doubling of sales, a successful TQM process can and should be in place such that it will continue in perpetuity, having a significant impact on both quality and earnings.

It is proposed that throughout this three-stage process, I work with senior and middle management to train and coach in TQM processes and principles and work with employees to help them learn what their roles in TQM are and how they can participate. My role will be that of trainer, coach, curmudgeon, critic, and devil's advocate, while helping the company into the adoption of TQM in its own ways. However, all of the work will be in the context of assisting the company in its efforts to implement its TQM program. In other words, my principal goal, beginning on the 1st day on, will be to work myself out of a job as quickly as possible.

METHODOLOGY

This proposal deals only with Stage 1, the design and delivery of a detailed 2-day TQM introductory program for the top 20 people in the firm. The purpose of the program will be to

- Explain TQM processes so that all managers speak the same language
- Ensure that all managers are familiar with the principles of TQM and have the opportunity to ask questions about the specifics of TQM as it applies to their areas of responsibility
- Assist senior management in enrolling all of the participants in the program and the values represented by TQM and assuage any fears or misgivings they may have about the process or how it may affect their jobs
- Provide the company's management with the opportunity to experience working with me and to gain an understanding about how I work and how my role in this process will evolve.

The specifics of what and how much additional involvement I would have in Stage 2 and Stage 3 efforts will be a result of this 2-day program.

TIMING AND RESPONSIBILITIES

Based on our preliminary discussions, it would seem that early July is the best time to deliver the 2-day introductory management program. I will perform all of the preparatory work and deliver the 2-day program myself. I will report directly to you in your role as CEO or to any other member of senior management that you may designate.

You may want to consider holding this program on a consecutive Friday and Saturday, preferably off-site at a proper business conference facility. I would be glad to work with the site manager to ensure that the facilities and necessary equipment are provided.

(continued)

Enclosed with this letter are two documents. A brief biographical sketch on my experience and qualifications and a draft outline of the proposed 2-day program.

ARRANGEMENTS FOR MY SERVICES

My professional fees for Stage 1 as proposed, including 2 to 3 days' preparation time and 1 day of follow-up consultation, will be $15,000. In addition to professional fees, I will charge back at cost my out-of-pocket expenses for office supplies, training materials and the like, telephone, and any travel connected with delivery of the program at a site outside the immediate area. Both professional fees and expenses are billed and are payable monthly as they are incurred.

Any other follow-up work related to Stage 2 and Stage 3 programs will be proposed and priced separately following the successful completion of Stage 1.

BENEFITS

Wendell, this is one of the most critical projects undertaken in the history of the firm. The successful development of TQM as an ongoing management philosophy and process at Worldwide Widgets will be a major factor in ensuring the firm's continued competitive advantage, distinctive competence, and successful growth into the next century and into the next generation of family management.

The benefits of this initial 2-day program will be the

- Opportunity for all managers to learn the principles and details of TQM as it should be applied at Worldwide Widgets
- Opportunity to discuss in an open forum issues and concerns about TQM's potential impact on the company
- Opportunity to enroll all of the company's managers in a total commitment to TQM on a consensus basis
- Opportunity to do so on a very cost effective basis for the firm; providing 20 managers with 2 days of TQM training for the fee proposed works out to about one-third the cost for similar packaged management programs held in major cities
- Opportunity to begin directing the company forward into its next successful stage of growth and development.

It also will provide you and your management with the opportunity to experience working with me so that you will be able to determine if I am the right agent to work with you long term in this quest. For me it will be an opportunity to learn more about Worldwide Widgets and to build effective working relationships with all of your managers; it will be a privilege to participate in the kickoff of so important a project for your firm.

Figure 4.1. Continued

I will call you in the next few days to answer any questions you or your staff may have and to ascertain how we should proceed. If you agree to this Stage 1 proposal, please sign one copy of this letter and return it to me so that I might begin my work. Thank you again for the opportunity to propose on this project.

Sincerely,

Renee Voltaire, Ph.D.
Professor of Logistics
Agreed to for Worldwide Widgets: _____
Date: _____

---

most complex, demanding, and thoroughly frustrating rules and regulations regarding formal proposals. In these situations, you may be asked to detail your fees by the hour or to submit detailed outlines of your final product or involved Gaant charts of your proposed work schedule. You may be asked to apply some bizarre formula to your base professional fees to calculate what you are authorized for your overhead and administrative costs related to the project. In fact, some of these public proposal documents are every bit as complicated as an application for a National Science Foundation (NSF) grant. If you have associated your practice with an existing, successful consulting firm, there are people on staff who know how to develop such proposals, and they can help you. If you are truly on your own, the best approach is to identify who within the client organization is administering such matters and *ask them* for samples of previously successful proposals or for any other information and material they can give you to help you in the process. Usually, if you turn on the charm, they will be more than willing to help.

Finally, do not forget that the written proposal is a *discussion document,* one that allows you to discover any misunderstandings about the issues and your approach and allows the client to modify what you have proposed. Both actions go a long way to ensure that you do get the job. However, the proposal must be followed by a phone call to initiate these conversations. Don't be fearful or shy. It's all part of the sales process and just one more opportunity to build an early positive relationship with your new client!

Oral Presentations

Earlier it was noted that to ensure a successful sale, never let anyone else do your selling for you. Such a person can't answer questions about your subject knowledge, can't detail the research you would do or the way you would do it, and can't relate your experience as you can. This leads to the fact that even with a formal written proposal, you are going to have to develop strong presentation skills to follow up and close the sale. Such skills are needed not only for selling the work up front but also for presenting your findings, conclusions, and recommendations later on. You may be required to deliver the results to a very large and powerful audience.

Another concern is the fact that many organizations are using a team approach to problem solving these days. For example, in the past, the director of training would recommend a particular firm or trainer to develop and deliver a package on supervisory skills to all first-time supervisors. Today, there is a good chance that in that same firm, the presentation is made to the director of training but also to a panel of those first-time supervisors who will be the recipients of the program. It will be the panel that decides who gets the training contract. As a result, you will need to pull together a strong oral presentation in support of the written proposal.

These situations are more common than you might imagine. Typically, when meeting with a prospective client for the first time, I am taken around the company; shown the plant floor, products, and processes; and introduced to senior managers in various functional areas, workers, and shift supervisors. It will be the consensus of the impressions I have made across the organization that will help me get the job. No longer does the work get sold solely in a private meeting in the president's office or with the executive committee of the board. On the other hand, such presentations all are additional opportunities for you to appear before the client, explain your thoughts and methods, and close the sale!

Here are some things you can do to ensure high levels of acceptance and success at these oral presentations:

Establish the Ground Rules. At the start of your presentation, review what you intend to do. Ask if there is anything else the audience would like you to cover. Check that you have the time allotted to make your presentation. Ask how the audience would like to handle questions. I prefer to make my presentation and then handle any and all queries. Some client cultures prefer interrupting your presentation frequently. Pace yourself so that you have adequate time reserved for questions.

Explain Things in Their Terms. Just because you're an academic, don't act like one. This presentation is not in front of your peers, and trying to impress the audience is only going to turn it off. Typically, these are practical people with real problems seeking straightforward solutions in their terms, solutions they can understand well enough to implement remedial actions. Although your audience wants to feel that you have the technical knowledge to help them, what they really are screening for is whether you are down to earth, sympathetic, and easy and fun to work with; they want to know if they can learn something from you and enjoy the relationship. So be clear in your own mind what your message at this meeting really is.

Use Visuals. Classroom skills are valuable in these oral presentations. Prepare a few key overhead transparencies. Keep them plain and simple in their message. Use them to repeat the key points you want to make about your proposal, your methodology, and the benefits.

Include Artwork. I work with a Macintosh Classic II and keep a lot of clip art in my files to make my overheads appear professionally developed. A logo here or there and a cute cartoon to help make a point add up to a personalized presentation that communicates you are all the things they are looking for: involved, caring, knowledgeable, humorous, and capable.

Acquire Infinite Patience. Just as in any instructional activity, maintain infinite patience. You are in a teaching mode. You know what you are proposing, why you are proposing it, and how it will help the client. The client doesn't know these things. Certainly, the president was impressed in his or her meeting with you, but now you must win over the other key people in the room and come across more skilled and sympathetic than the other three consultants with whom they are talking. Answer every single question they ask. Volunteer as much additional information as you can. Help them to understand and feel good about the way you would work with them and address their issues.

Ask for the Business. The oral presentation following the written proposal is usually *your last best shot* at making the sale. Don't be bashful. When you have finished your presentation, tell the audience how much you would value the relationship, how interesting their problems and opportunities are to you professionally, and how much you would enjoy working with them. Ask for the business!

Client Attitudes

It is helpful to have a perspective on the expectations your client may have for their consultant. Just a few years ago, it was common to come across a small to midsize firm that had never used consultants and certainly had never considered engaging a scholar from the local university. In such instances, it was a straightforward effort to explain what consultants

Table 4.2 Clients' Attitudes Toward Consultants

Used to Be	Today
Client sought out brand name firms	Client looks for consultants with specific expertise
Client took brand name firms for granted	Client often inquires about academic affiliations and research efforts
Client awarded contracts casually	Client often sets up competitive bidding
Add-on business was the norm	Each phase of the work goes to the most qualified consultant
Client engaged outside help readily	Client develops more internal teams and task forces to use all the MBA talent paid for over the years

did, how they worked, and what to expect. It was really just one more exercise in educating your market to your services and their benefits.

Today, this is no longer the case. Most companies have had experience with one type of consultant or another. And depending on the outcome, certain expectations now exist. If the client had a bad experience, there is enormous skepticism for you to overcome. If it was a very positive experience, then the client expects that you will perform exactly as that other consultant did, whether you are aware of the previously used methods and style or not. An overview of clients' expectations and values relative to their consultants can best be summarized as shown in Table 4.2.

Setting Your Fee Structure

As a professional consultant, my fees are my livelihood. I take them very seriously and work hard at the art of collecting them on a timely basis. Unless you were born to wealth and privilege or are a full, tenured professor at the Harvard Business School, you should learn how these matters are handled.

As few scholars go into teaching for the money associated with the profession, most of those I have worked with in a consulting relationship are terribly inexperienced about what they should charge for their consulting efforts. There is a strong, lemminglike urge to give it away. Don't do that! If for no other reason, think about the cost of your education, the final price of that doctorate. Good grief! It ought to start paying back at some time in your career. Perhaps now is the moment!

The true value of your consulting work is calibrated from two sources: what you believe your time is worth and what the market will bear.

What You Believe. What is the value of your time? Professional consultants calculate their net hours available for consulting (after subtracting administrative time and at least one-third of the year for marketing efforts, vacation, sick leave, etc.) and dividing that number of hours into the amount of income they need and feel they are worth. A simplistic example would work as follows: There are approximately 22 working days in a month. There are 8 hours in a working day; therefore, there are between 176 and 180 billable hours in a month. For a full-time consultant, one-third of that time should be devoted to new business development. One day a week, or 24 hours per month, evaporates into administrative time, leaving about 100 billable hours in a typical month.

If the consultant wants to earn $120,000 a year in which there are 1,200 billable hours, then he or she must bill out his or her time at $100 an hour. But this will only gross the $120,000. The consultant also must pay a part-time clerical assistant; rent on the office; monthly payments for the computer, laser printer, and other paraphernalia in the office; and $400 a month for the car lease. These operating expenses increase the consultant's gross requirements approximately 40% from $10,000 a month to $14,000 a month, translating to an hourly billing rate of $140 an hour or $1,120 per day to realize the $120,000 per year. It really is that simple.

What the Market Bears. Senior partners in large, established consulting firms, especially strategy boutiques and Big 6 accounting firms, charge between $3,000 and $5,000 per day. Roughly half of that amount goes to the firm's overhead, the posh offices downtown, the tasteful furnishings, the limo for the managing partner, the advertising and research staffs, and all of that expensive indirect marketing. Fortune 1000 clients can and do pay such fees. This should set an upper limit on what you can ask for your time, although true superstar scholars such as Porter and Kantor of the Harvard Business School have been known to charge as much as $25,000 a day or $10,000 for a 90-minute speech. Is this, then, what our intrepid full-time consultant should quote? Not at all. First, as a solo practitioner, the consultant's clients probably hire him or her because they know it will be far less expensive than A. T. Kearney. Second, the consultant is not working with Fortune 1000 firms, because the scope of their jobs is too large for a one-person practice. He or she is probably working with smaller, family-owned and -managed businesses or industrials with annual sales of $25 million or less a year. These businesses can't afford $3,000 a day for consultants. As a result, the marketplace can and will bear anywhere from $800 a day to $2,000 a day for independent consultants, MBAs with experience and powerful references from satisfied clients.

Although these machinations are fairly easy for the full-time consultant, where does the part-time practice of the consulting scholar fit in? How do you price yourself if the university only allows 1 day a week for consulting? Or do you believe that is all the time you can budget for such efforts? Many peers tell me that they perceive themselves as a teacher/researcher first, and a consultant only in their spare time.

All this is important, but are you worth any less than the hypothetical full-time consultant we used for our pricing example above? Just because you chose scholarship, science, and the search for truth shouldn't prohibit you from earning $120,000 a year as well. How do we calculate it? Easy. If you are earning, say, $50,000 a year as an associate professor at school, and you have 1 day a week available for consulting and there are 52 weeks in a year, then you should charge approximately $1,000 a day for your consulting effort. However, life is never *that* simple. Even if you perform most of your marketing and public relations efforts during the other four days of the week, you probably won't generate exactly 52 days a year in billable work. You have to think about travel time, sick time, vacations, and attending academic conferences. You also have to offset the cost of your consulting equipment, fax machine, cellular telephone for the car, calling cards, and marketing brochures. It all comes out to roughly double your $1,000-a-day fee to ensure that you gross $2,000 a day when you consult. When compared with what the hypothetical consultant is charging, without even an MBA, $2,000 a day isn't that far from the competition or from what the market will bear. Your research and the in-depth understanding you have of your field and related areas surely is worth that amount.

Finally, it helps to know who the competition is. A case in point from my own experience is that I received a call from a large financial institution based in New Orleans a few years ago. They had read several of my articles and wanted to know if I would come to New Orleans for a 1-day seminar with their executive committee to discuss the potential impact of pending legislation. The senior vice president who called me explained that he would appreciate knowing what I would charge for such a meeting. My thought process went as follows: taking a day off and flying to New Orleans and then flying back is a real inconvenience; however, I can prep on the plane. If they are talking to other people, it must be McKinsey and/or Booz, Allen. If they are asked to send a senior partner out for 1 day, they will quote at least $5,000, and probably more. As a result, I quoted $5,000 plus expenses. My logic was that I really had other things to do so if I overpriced myself and didn't get the job, it was no great loss; however, if I was up against McKinsey, then I might actually appear very cost effective to the client. And, as the Fates would have it, they called back an hour later and gave me the work. They got their money's worth, and for $5,000 a day and first-class travel, I can deal with the inconvenience of altering my schedule!

The opposite side of this example is that many large firms will reduce their normal fees significantly, almost give the business away, when they really want a particular job or a specific client affiliation. This is called "pro bono" work, and as solo consultants working only part-time, it is not something we can afford to do very often. A Big 6 accounting firm such as Peat, Marwick may choose to write off the introductory phase of a major job to get to phase two or three, where they can make more than their usual profit margin. But they are doing this day in and day out and can afford to average their fees out over the long haul. The difficult decision for the consulting scholar is in the case of a truly needy client, a small firm with few resources, one that cannot afford your usual $2,000 a day fee. The issues here are as follows: Do you want the work? Is it a really unusual or challenging issue? Can you learn a lot from the experience? Can you honestly help the client and will he or she make an outstanding reference for you 1 year down the road? From time to time the answers to these questions will fall out in such a way that you take the assignment, perhaps charging only $1,000 a day or giving free days along the way until the problem is solved. Other times, you may not have the days available to do the work or you may have other more lucrative projects under way. Each incident is a judgment call. Just be sure to return your calls from New Orleans!

Keeping Perspective

Now that you have visions of sugar plums dancing in your head, it is necessary to step back and put a perspective on what you can and cannot accomplish financially as a part-time

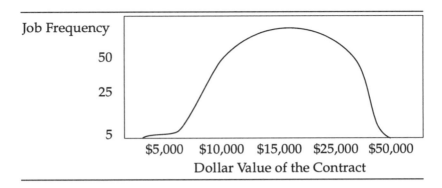

Figure 4.2. Frequency and Value of Contracts

consulting scholar. If I were to draw a bell curve of all the consulting projects I had ever sold, it might look something like Figure 4.2.

In summary, then, while you may not accept too many assignments for $5,000, as they are too time consuming to set up, perform, and debrief on, you will sell and deliver any number of $10,000-$15,000 contracts on your own; and occasionally, you will be rewarded with a $25,000-$30,000 assignment. But in the end, there are apt not to be too many sales beyond $40,000-$50,000, simply because they are too large for you to perform on your own. You will have to subcontract or partner with others. In the end, you will see only a portion of the total amount of the proposal for yourself. If, however, you find you are able to develop longer-term relationships and are frequently asked to bid on very large projects, you may want to consider seriously building up a larger firm or going full-time and foregoing your academic efforts in the near future.

Getting Paid and Payment Schedules

Just as there are any number of permutations on a project, there are also permutations on how you can get paid for your consulting efforts. Most often, consultants charge on a monthly basis for professional fees and related expenses.

One-time payments for an entire project also are acceptable to clients if the duration of the project is short and the deliverables are quite specific, say, a 2-week job to evaluate an art portfolio or 3 days to prepare for and act as an expert witness for a law firm. In such cases, a single invoice including all related expenses is common practice.

Retainers are fees that have been divided into monthly amounts. In a way it permits the client to pay over time. For example, on a typical $50,000 contract, the monthly billings might be $5,000, $15,000, $20,000, $5,000, and $5,000. However, the client would prefer to pay an even amount of $10,000 a month for 5 months so he or she can better manage cash flow or profitability. In such cases, it is important that you keep track of the actual work performed versus the fees received so that you can reconcile what you have done with what you have been paid. It is important to ensure the client does not overpay and that you do not work for free.

Monthly retainers are a very nice way to be compensated. If you have been working with a client for a while and the trust levels are high, you may propose, say, $60,000 worth of projects over the next year. Rather than wait for each project to start and end, you ask your client to put you on the payroll for $5,000 a month, and you perform the projects in the best sequence for the client. You must be careful to document what has been done and what is owed on a monthly basis, but if you have two or three clients on such monthly retainers, together with your paycheck from the university, it is the best of all possible worlds. The catch is that when working under such retainers, it is all too easy to forget that there is no guarantee anyone will pick up your contract again next year, and you may forget to perform business development on a regular basis. Beware: Consulting clients do not know the meaning of the word *tenure*.

Contingency fees are generally frowned on professionally. These payments generally are *contingent on* some future outcome, a return to profitability, the goods will sell at the appraisal price, the advertising campaign will be a success, and so on. It has been my experience over the years that there are far too many things that can go wrong in a contingency arrangement, things well outside the consultant's control. All too often, these contracts place the consultant at odds with his or her client and the threat of litigation looms over the relationship. It is my opinion that such situations should never be allowed to arise, especially when the consultant is also a well-known scholar.

If a prospect insists that you work on a contingency basis, my advice is not to do so. However, if you must, be certain you have documented carefully exactly what you are to do, what the expected results of your effort are to be, how that will be quantified and measured, and who and when the measurement will take place, so that you can be compensated fairly and on a timely basis. But already you can sense how complicated these contingency agreements can become.

Finally, we come to the turnaround situation, when you agree to work for a firm or a family that truly is on the naked edge. Every turnaround specialist I know, negotiates that so long as they are working to save the company, they get paid their fees *weekly* and at the head of the line. And the first week they do not get paid immediately, they stop work. Business is business, even in life-and-death situations.

Marketing Resources

A final issue under this topic of selling is if you should take the time and spend the money to develop slick brochures about your practice. Do you need formal business cards and stationery separate from your college letterhead? It has been my experience that if produced tastefully all this can help to communicate a professionalism about your consulting. Furthermore, there may be some very real reasons for separate cards and stationery. A number of universities take the posture that you are their employee, first and foremost. They limit the time you are authorized to consult off campus. A number of other schools demand that you tithe up to 30% of your consulting income with the university, even when the client contacted you outside the academic institution! Although I am not suggesting that you evade your employer's tithing policies, if all of the correspondence and working documents you produce for a client are on university letterhead, it is very difficult to explain why you should not tithe your fees if that is the policy.

With state-of-the-art word processing and a laser printer, it shouldn't take you very long or cost you a great deal to develop a few basic marketing materials.

Calling Cards. Most printing shops prefer that you order 500 to 1,000 cards at a time because they only make money on volume production. Still, 500 cards shouldn't cost more than $30 to $40 if that, and 1,000 cards will last longer than your new Volvo! Before you place such an order, be certain you have an address and a phone and fax number that will be valid for a while. Order your cards with a crisp, classic typeface, one that communicates conservative professionalism. Have them printed on heavy stock, not cheap, thin card paper. Calling cards are a tactile experience. Unless you have a Freudian thing about colors, order your cards on white stock, not mauve, or beige, or gray.

Stationery. In keeping with the image you want to project with your calling cards, order plain white stock of at least 20-pound paper. If you want to create a logo, keep it simple. *M&A* is something I created on my computer and use for Metzger & Associates. In addition to letterhead, you will need second sheets, and many of my colleagues also order report covers with their logos.

Brochures. Brochures are very personal and really a matter of style. For a few hours' work, you can design and develop a nice four-page brochure that explains who you are, what your expertise is, and what services you provide; have it printed on 11-by-17 stock in 80-pound weight. You will be able to provide prospects with a professional piece that communicates you are an experienced consultant with something to offer. Printing 2,000 such four-page pieces shouldn't cost more than a few hundred dollars.

Consulting Curriculum Vitae. Whether you develop separate brochures about your practice or not, you need to create a short, one-page piece about yourself that stresses your consulting experience and accomplishments. This is something you can store on your computer to use whenever you are sending out a proposal or responding to an inquiry. By not having it printed, you maintain the flexibility you need to modify it, depending on the message you want to convey. But a curriculum vitae (CV) is something you will find yourself using weekly for one situation or another. Figure 4.3 presents an example of a one-page consulting CV.

The best way I can think of to summarize this discussion about marketing your consulting activities is to realize that we are halfway through the book and we're just getting off marketing and sales to start discussing the consulting process and its nuances and your new business efforts. Fully half of your consulting efforts will be identifying and selling clients. You can never develop a practice or reap its benefits and rewards without an enormous, if not all-consuming, marketing effort. It will be frustrating most of the time, infuriating some of the time, but it all pays back with the beginning of a new client relationship and the challenge of new problems and opportunities.

Elizabeth G. Furgeson, Ph.D., RN, CMC

Elizabeth G. Furgeson is managing principal of Furgeson & Associates, an Omaha-based consulting firm serving the health care industry throughout the Midwest. Dr. Furgeson has been working with the CEOs and human resource directors from a wide range of health care organizations to develop and sustain the managerial and supervisorial skills of clinical and professional staff. Clients have included 7 of the 10 largest hospitals in the Midwest and dozens of small, local institutions, psychiatric clinics, and nursing homes.

Dr. Furgeson also is associate professor of management and organization at the Edsel School of Business Administration, University of North Northeast Nebraska, where she lectures in organization design, work design, and leadership. She is associated with the university's Center for Applied Research and regularly performs field studies in leadership and effective organization design.

Dr. Furgeson began her career in health care as a registered nurse and worked in the trauma center of three major Midwest hospitals, including the Mayo Clinic, before pursuing her career in academia and consulting. She performed her undergraduate studies at Northwestern University and her graduate studies at the Colorado School of Road and Mines, where she earned a Ph.D. in quantum physics.

Dr. Furgeson is a member of the Executive Committee of the Organizational Behavior Division of the National Academy of Management and a certified management consultant (CMC) with the Institute of Management Consultants.

Figure 4.3. Sample One-Page Consulting Curriculum Vitae

5 | The Process Perspective

Given that by now you have had some success in your marketing, there are three basic perspectives you need to gain. Each of the next three chapters is devoted to (a) how to start-up and manage a project to satisfy the needs of a client, (b) how to operate a successful ongoing consulting practice, and (c) how to develop that practice into a sustaining business over longer periods of time, particularly if you have decided to replace your teaching career with one in consulting. These perspectives are process, operations, and strategic.

The consulting process is much like any other. There is a beginning, a middle passage, and an end. It's an unusually exciting process, however, and this chapter passes through a typical client relationship, noting a few things you will need to focus on along the way to ensure a successful project and, perhaps, some additional consulting work.

Beginning a New Relationship

Starting a relationship with a new client has always been the real challenge for me. To begin, there is a need to observe, learn, and understand the organization's culture. Successful consultants have already begun to do this when they visit the client company for the first time in a business development role.

Performing Research. Often, if it is a public company, there are articles and newspaper stories available about recent events, successes, and failures; new products or services; or a new CEO or majority shareholder. And when you went for the initial interview, you asked the CEO's secretary for a copy of the latest annual report. Failing that, you obtained a copy from a local brokerage firm or you wrote the company secretary requesting a copy. For privately held firms or nonprofit organizations, usually there is some form of annual report they prepare for benefactors, public relations, or other purposes. These tend to be readily available. An often overlooked source of sound intelligence is that of competitors. Talking to the sales force, customers, or management of a rival firm often can provide extremely valuable information and different perspectives.

Defining the Culture. When the consultant enters the company's offices, he or she is looking for telltale signs of the culture. Are doors open or closed, are people dressed casually or in white shirts and red ties? Is clerical staff allowed personal items on its desks? Are the premises bright, well lit, and furnished with modern or period furniture? Is there an executive dining room separate from the cafeteria? Are there reserved parking spaces? Is it a union or nonunion shop? Do the employees appear happy and vivacious or grim and subdued? All of these easily observed phenomena are clues to the atmosphere within the client's organization.

Learning the Power and Politics. Along with scoping the client's culture, values, and attitudes, you want to open a discussion tactfully with your principal contact regarding the power and the politics of the organization. Just because the president urged that you be hired and you won the contract doesn't ensure that the six divisional vice presidents want you or any other outsider around. Perhaps the chair was out of town, and the CEO slipped you in before anyone noticed. Not very likely, but you should be political enough to check it out.

There also are some basic questions you need to ask to understand how the organization gets things done. How are decisions made? By senior individuals or by committees? By management or the board? By powerful members of the family or key shareholders?

Locating Allies and Silent Agendas. A major part of your initial intelligence work should deal with the identification of those senior people in the organization who support your proposal and wish to help you; individuals who want to see you and your project succeed, and those who are most threatened by the work; and key people who can and just might mug you in the elevator! All this might seem a bit paranoid, especially if all you are selling is a training program, economic data, or your personal research on shale strata, but often there are uncanny parallels between the corporate world and academia. Someone shut the director of training out of the loop, who had been planning for several months to do this training himself or herself. The director of finance is upset because no one consulted him or her, yet most of the people going through this program are under his or her supervision. The manager of the local plant expected his or her spouse, a consultant, to be "wired" for the project. The executive committee that hired you already has concluded that the president is a dolt, and it is just waiting for your report to confirm that earlier conclusion.

There are dozens of situations in every organization that can have a supportive or destructive impact on your innocent little project. It shouldn't take you too many projects to realize that when things have deteriorated to the point at which an outside specialist is brought in, someone feels threatened, and that someone thinks the consultant is going to make him or her look bad. Check it out—quietly!

Scoping the Project. Another early step in your new relationship is to further scope out the job. It may seem clear that what is to be done has already been reviewed and accepted in the proposal, but now that you are on the payroll and inside the company, there may be information that you didn't have before—problems no one spoke about earlier. There may be more to the issues than what the president shared with you. After reviewing all these possibilities, just what are you going to do for the budget that has been approved? Who should know about that? Who might be working with you and assisting from inside the company? What is his or her opinion? Are there areas or issues such a person feels you may have over-looked or not thought about? All this is critical information needed to develop a final project outline and work plan, whether you are designing a training program or a complex employee attitudinal survey.

Defining Your Role. Are you a partner with the client or on your own, working in relative solitude? Whose agenda pre-vails, yours or the clients'? Are they content to let you develop the data, prove your hypothesis, and make recommendations or do they want to be included in every step of your work and in your thought processes? What are their expectations? Again, this may be a facet of the work that was covered in the proposal, but it won't do any harm, and it could do a great deal of good for you, to review these aspects of the assign-ment. Some clients may want you highly visible around the organization for shock purposes, others may want you work-ing off-site anonymously.

Enlisting Support. How much help—facilities and resources —will the client contribute? If you have a great many inter-views to perform, is a conveniently located office or confer-ence room available to you? Do you have free access to all areas in the building or plant? Has your sponsor sent out a memo introducing you to the organization and explaining your assignment? Figure 5.1 presents a sample introductory memo. Is there clerical staff available to do typing or copying work for you on-site? Can the client provide you with access to an office, a telephone extension where you can be reached, and a PC while you are working on-site? If you have to travel

---

MEMORANDUM

TO: All Curators—Museum of Modern Antiquities

FROM: Sy Sclerotic, Chairman

SUBJECT: Dr. Bruce Wayne

As you know, the museum has not experienced the level of visitors this year that we have enjoyed in the past. Recently, the board of governors of the museum engaged Dr. Bruce Wayne, professor of history and crowd control, from State University, for his expertise in antiquities marketing and traffic improvement programs.

Dr. Wayne has assisted a number of other museums throughout the Midwest to improve their traffic levels and is well known in his field of expertise.

In the next few days, Dr. Wayne will be contacting each of you to obtain your views and insights to the challenges facing us. I want to thank you in advance for your cooperation, and I assure you that anything you may share with Dr. Wayne will remain in his confidence.

While working with us, I have authorized Dr. Wayne to use the old fossil storeroom in the west wing of the basement as his temporary office. You may contact him there on extension 335.

Figure 5.1. Memo of Introduction

NOTE: This is a memo that Dr. Wayne asked his client to send out on his behalf.

---

from out of town, is there a company apartment or quarters where you might stay that would save the firm outrageous hotel bills? Is there a company car available to you for local mobility?

Ensuring You Get Paid—Properly. One thing I am always careful to learn is the correct procedure for getting consultant invoices paid on a timely basis. Who in the accounting department handles such things? What format is needed? What does accounting want in the way of backup documentation, receipts, and so on and in how many copies? In short, how can you ensure that your invoice gets to the head of the queue and your check is sent out promptly? It never hurts to ask.

Another aspect of the startup process is to have candid conversations with your sponsor regarding who the nay-sayers to this project are and how they can be brought into the process. Often enlisting them as part of a task force or a steering committee can provide them with new insights that will turn them around or at least neutralize their resistance.

Establishing Hypotheses. What really is out of kilter? Are you sure it is the obvious? I have numerous war stories about clients who hired me because they thought it was a marketing problem when, in fact, it was any number of decision-making process problems that undermined sales. Is the issue functionally localized or systemic? Is it geographically local or worldwide? What are its true impacts on the organization, on customers, on employees? To begin helping the client you need to gather enough data to establish some form of hypothesis that can be factually and scientifically proven or disproven. If anyone should know how to approach this, it should be a scholar such as yourself. If anyone can screw that process up, it also will be the scholar. Where we tend to get in trouble as consultants is that we forget we are on financial and time budgets. How long and how much this work will cost must be scoped out up front. Then a rigorous work schedule must be committed to, or the project will take too long, cost too much, and you will have lost a client and hurt your reputation as a consulting scholar.

A major insight into this problem has to do with data development. In the real world there is a great deal of imperfection, especially with respect to data. There is too little of them, and what are held are squirrelly, at best. Yet decisions must be made and the business process must move forward. In scholarship, often we take months or years to develop our data in the ever-intoxicating search for truth. Ours is a process steeped in a luxury of time that our clients have never had and cannot accept. So often the consulting scholar is intimidated to move ahead by questionable data. It is your ability to determine just what data you need and how imperfect they can be—and still provide you with valid conclusions—that can determine your success as a consultant.

Developing Data and Sharing Discovery. What internal data exist relative to your project? How credible are they? Who develops them off what database and who in the organization uses those reports? What do they think of the reports' validity? What kinds of decisions are made with the data? By whom? How timely are the data? How timely should they be to have value for your project? What external data exist in libraries, brokerage firms, with industry analysts, in industry associations, and in the economics department? Are there client staff assigned to work with you to develop these data? Does management want a report on your progress? Do they want to have a say in what data are sourced and eventually used? How should you provide progress reports to your sponsor or the steering committee for the project?

Managing the Process

Interpreting the Data. What do the data mean—to you as an independent observer? To the client? To the nay-sayer you enrolled to help you develop the data? What other interpretations might there be? How do these findings support or contradict your hypothesis and the client's assumptions— about the issues and their cause? If you were the client, how would you react or feel given what you now know? Is there a major surprise involved? Will someone lose face or risk embarrassment? What should you do about it, if anything?

Progress Reports. Many young consulting scholars I talk with are under the misconception that a consulting project is ordered by the client, performed by the consultant, and the results provided in some lengthy report. Although that might have been the process 10 or 20 years ago, it is not the process today. If we have learned anything as consultants over the last few decades, it is that successful consulting relationships hinge on satisfied clients. In turn, satisfied clients feel that they own the project, the process, and the results, and that they have played a major role in defining and resolving the issues. It is only through the creation of such an atmosphere that the client will gain the commitment needed successfully to introduce solutions and needed change. So the questions you need to ask of your client are the following: How often does the client want to know how you are doing? What is a reasonable passage of time before you report? What exactly would they like to know? In what form should it be delivered —a brief memo or an oral report? To the president or a steering committee? And, remember, throughout these periodic progress reports, the client may ask a lot of questions, not because he or she distrusts you or your methods, but because the client genuinely wants to learn more about the problems and possible solutions. At all costs, you must avoid personalizing what seems to be challenges to what you are doing and how you are doing it at this stage.

Midcourse Corrections. Often in a successful consulting project there are midcourse corrections to the hypothesis or the conclusions from the data developed. Based on any discrepancies between the results of the research and the original hypothesis, what might change? How should it change? What are the implications? These are issues to explain candidly to the client and sound dialogue should take place. In the example I gave earlier, when the client came to recognize that too few decisions were being delegated to permit sales to occur at a level expected from the latest marketing promotions, the entire project took on a different focus and track, one that had to do with the overall organization structure and approval authorities rather than passing judgment on the competence of the marketing director. Although not every project uncovers such surprises, there must be enough flexibility built into the process that you can discuss such issues with your client, turn things in a different direction, and still have the budget to complete the work.

Another form of midcourse correction is that of the cost or time overrun. Chapter 6 introduces a number of time and expense forms that every consultant must keep. They not only justify how you spend the client's monies but also create a paper trail that documents cost and time overruns that, more often than not, are created by the client. When you recalculate a project and see that you have been delayed 2 weeks or that what the client has asked for in terms of additional work or research will cost another $10,000, it is time to address these issues head-on and renegotiate the contract. The client will understand and usually will agreee to the time extention or the extra funds, but be sure you have it documented and can demonstrate that the excesses rest with the client's organization and not your own lack of discipline.

Reaching Conclusions. What's the best way to close in on the truth? How much should the client be involved? Is the client's environment sufficiently objective to include key people in the process? How might such objectivity be developed if it does not naturally occur in the organization? Who might be considered "the winner" and "the loser" as a result of your conclusions? How will these people handle the information? Will this create more divisiveness or actually resolve an issue everyone already suspected? What is the best way to present these conclusions and to what possible solutions do they lead?

Developing Solutions. One of the simplest yet most deadly mistakes consultants make is to develop what I call mom-and-pop solutions to resolve complex issues in dynamic organizations versus "General Motors" solutions to help small organizations with limited resources. Although the former may seem elegant in their simplicity, the odds are your client's large, geographically dispersed and politically sophisticated culture will require something more than a new organization structure. It also will require a change plan, change agents,

Table 5.1 Midproject Progress Report

1. Have key client personnel been informed of my work? Does everyone have a copy of the proposal who needs one? Has everyone been effectively briefed?
2. Have subcontractors, suppliers, customers, or consultants working on other projects been informed of what they need to know?
3. Have I been reviewing my preliminary analyses of the data with the client?
4. Are my conclusions sound? Am I testing my findings with key client personnel?
5. Are the recommendations I am formulating appropriate for the client, given limitations and opportunities?
6. Am I spending enough time on alternate solutions with a cost-benefit focus?
7. Am I incorporating the client's ideas, conclusions, and recommendations to ensure ownership?
8. Am I close to agreement from key managers as to the best solution?
9. Am I on time and on budget?
10. Am I keeping track of changes to the work plan as it may affect the budget later?

and specific unit-based organizational objectives to be completed and accepted successfully. Conversely, if your client is a small art and antiquities gallery in Greenwich Village, to suggest such an involved change process, one that requires resources far beyond the limits of the client, would be a great disservice. So the scope of the solution is important. So, too, is the direction of change. By now you have been inside the organization long enough to have a good sense of the culture and the values held by most managers and employees. Prescribing solutions that run counter to the culture can be just as doomed to failure as solutions that are too simplistic. If the best solution is to move in a counter cultural direction, how might this be done in stages? or in different parts of the organization in less threatening ways? Table 5.1 is a midproject progress report that you can administer yourself to evaluate how the project is going.

End Game: Managing Change

Presenting Conclusions. To some extent, the issues around the presentation of your conclusions are similar to those of progress reports. What is to be presented? To whom? And in what format? If there is to be a final written report, one of the best questions to ask is simply, "How many copies?" This is important as you may want to present your findings with a slightly different spin to the board of directors from the one presented to the marketing committee. Ask your sponsor. What issues might the board focus on? What kinds of questions might members ask? Does the board like visual or oral presentations? Should members receive a summary in advance of the meeting?

Similarly sensitive issues exist when presenting conclusions to management. How can it be done to preserve objectivity? If one individual or department may appear at fault, is there some way to tone down that potential embarrassment? Does senior management want those people protected? Would exposing them in a particularly harsh light really resolve anything? All are issues to consider when delivering the mail.

Selling Alternatives. Think through what you are recommending. By now you should know enough about the culture to know what is and is not saleable. What alternatives might you develop and hold in reserve? For example, when performing organizational audits, I always include in my questionnaire queries that allow me to report the 10 items the organization would most want changed and the 10 items the organization would least like to see changed. Such data allow a broad range of decisions to be made and help the client learn where dangerous areas of resistance may exist.

Enlisting Client Ownership. Depending on how much the client has been involved in research and discovery, he or she will sense some level of ownership at this point. One way to facilitate this bias is to allow the client some part of the presentation of conclusions. It is at such times, often, that your greatest detractor will end up your strongest supporter. The more the client feels this sense of ownership, the greater the chances that real, positive change can and will occur toward resolving the issues.

Energizing the Client for Change. Perhaps the greatest area where clients are unable to help themselves is in the area of change management and in understanding the change process. For one thing, managing a major change program is a full-time job, not something clients can assign to executives on a part-time basis while still holding them accountable for their daily work. Second, clients traditionally are focused on command-and-control functions and processes, not those of change. There may be little familiarity with change concepts, especially in smaller, less sophisticated organizations. Finally, even if human resource management (HRM) demands it be allowed to manage the planned changes, beware that the HRM staff, even with all its MBAs, has the real-time experience needed to get the job done effectively. Most often, even when I am not scheduled to implement the needed solutions or when the client insists on doing his or her own change work, I suggest the opportunity to hold a few sessions on change. Often this is just the opportunity needed to help the client realize that it is not something that can be performed alone, that the CEO must be highly visible and seen to support and drive the changes proposed, and that there is a skill and expertise required from outside the organization.

Another ploy to ensure that effective change occurs is one Tom Cummings of the Center for Effective Organization (CEO) at USC and I employed when introducing self-managed work groups to a major profit center of a leading-money center bank. We knew the process threatened many midlevel managers and there were solid blocks of resistance to the concept. So we offered to help only those department heads who volunteered to attempt the change in management policy. No one was forced to change. Over time, those department heads

Table 5.2 Project Close-Out Checklist

---

1. Do I have an appropriate plan for the client that describes implementation steps, roles, responsibilities, and critical milestone dates?
2. Have I taken training needs into consideration along with exposure to sensitivity instruction in change management?
3. Have I developed a progress evaluation and monitoring system for the client to track successful remedial programs?
4. Is there a system in place to track and quantify project cost savings or additional revenues?
5. Were overall project objectives achieved? If not, why not?
6. What overall learning can I gain from this project? What can the client learn from it? Is there a case to be developed here?
7. Am I tuned into buying signals from the client relative to add-on business?

---

that cooperated were given recognition and reward by senior management. This led to the clear communication of what was now acceptable performance, and soon, other managers were coming forward wanting to get on the train before it left the station. Such almost passive-reactive implementation may take a great deal more time, but the change outcome is more sure. Table 5.2 is a checklist to use in wrapping up a project.

Selling Add-On Contracts. You have been working now for a number of weeks with the client. They have come to know you, and you them. Now comes a pregnant moment, one that can lead to real success as a consultant. It is time to *sell more work*. If you have gained the client's trust and respect based on your methods and objectivity and your technical expertise, you should be able to sell an add-on contract to implement the solutions you are about to recommend, to research new issues that arose as a result of your first-phase work, or to begin a totally new study regarding a different problem uncovered in a different part of the organization. Over the years, while I have sold more strategic planning studies than any other type of job, the vast majority of my fees have been derived from the add-on contracts to implement a permanent planning process, to perform an organizational audit, or to market research—not from the strategy work per se. You need to ask yourself how to get them to say yes again. What is a logical next step? How can you leverage your newfound credibility and friendship? How might the partnership continue? See Figure 5.2 for an example of an add-on proposal letter.

Saying Goodbye. Most successful consultants develop relationships with clients that extend for several years. Such a relationship may be from a series of major contracts, one tied on after another. Or it can derive from a shadow relationship whereby you are on call for several days a month without anything specific of note. However, sooner or later, no matter how close the relationship, there comes a time to say goodbye and to get out! Often that may be when the accountants point out your total cumulative consulting fees over the past 5 years. Or maybe there is a change of leadership, management, or ownership in the company. Or, one hopes, it will be the result of all the positive contributions you have made so that there are no major new issues to conquer for the moment. Whatever the cause, it is time to go. So leave! Don't get maudlin, don't expect a farewell party, don't look for a lot of collective thanks. Just say good-bye! This shouldn't mean that you won't be back, it just means that there is nothing significant for you to do for the moment.

Maintaining Contacts. And the way you ensure that you will be called back, sooner or later, is through maintaining contact with the key people you have developed relationships with. Send the client articles, speeches, and newspaper clippings on relevant topics; add a short note: "Thinking of you" or "This is what we talked about in our last meeting." At least once a quarter call the client. Invite key people to lunch, have something to say to them, about their industry or their business or their competition. The image to portray is one of an interested expert, standing by and ready to be of help again when needed.

September 3, 1993

Mr. Sy Sclerotic
Chairman of the Board of Trustees
Museum of Modern Antiquities
Anytown, AK 98770

Dear Sy:

It was good meeting with you and the board this past week. This letter is to review our work to date and to outline the ideas we shared with the board.

WORK COMPLETED TO DATE

As you know, I spent most of last month interviewing all of the curators and department heads in the museum, reviewing your traffic levels on a quarterly basis for the past 3 years, and analyzing your exhibit promotions. I also analyzed the promotions and the timing of the exhibits of other museums and art galleries in the metropolitan area.

As a result of this research, I provided the board with an analysis of the causes for the drop in the museum's traffic these past 18 months.

WORK IN PROCESS

As a result of that report, I proposed to the board that I perform some community attitudinal surveys and a series of focus group roundtables with those psychographic segments of the populace tending to place value in art, history, and music. The survey was designed and mailed to 3000 residents last week. The first five focus groups have been conducted with PTA members, single parents under 40, minority business owners, patrons of PBS, and sustaining donors to the museum. The remaining focus group sessions will be completed before the end of this month, and the completed results of the attitudinal survey should be available in about 6 weeks.

WORK TO BE ACCOMPLISHED

As a result of these efforts, Sy, and as I explained to the board last week, I believe that the long-term solution to the museum's waning traffic patterns rests in the development of dynamic, youth-oriented programs and facilities on the museum's 50-acre grounds. To that end, this letter is to propose that I meet with Ten Flags—Montezuma's Revenge Corporation on behalf of the museum to draft a plan for a series of high-speed, dangerous rides and attractions to be constructed next to the museum over the ensuing 10 months. The projected sale of museum T-shirts and "brontosaurus burgers"

Figure 5.2. Sample Add-On Letter

alone should improve revenues 500% in 2 years and may actually improve visits to the museum ever so slightly.

My professional fees for representing the museum in these negotiations would be $50,000 plus out-of-pocket expenses for related costs.

Sy, it continues to be a pleasure working with you and the board, and it is an honor to help the museum regain its share of market in the community's entertainment attractions.

Sincerely,

Bruce Wayne, Ph.D.
Professor of History and Crowd Control
State University

6 | The Operations Perspective

Υ ou've been marketing your consulting services aggressively. After 9 months, you have three clients and two interesting projects; one may lead to a follow-up contract to perform some action research and another is excellent material for a case write-up. You also are making $5,000 a month over and above your academic salary, and it feels good—really good! The problem is that you have another major proposal in the offing that not only will generate enormous fees for you but also will bankrupt your available time. Now, what do you do?

This is the dilemma many, many consulting scholars find themselves unprepared for. Fortunately, there are a number of alternative solutions. This chapter presents the alternative choices for you and explores in detail the operational perspective of managing and developing your own consulting firm on a full-time basis. Several colleagues of mine like consulting but don't want to give up their academic lives. They enjoy being tenured, being addressed as "Professor," and being associated with a respected institution. So they put constraints on the kind of consulting they will do and exercise tremendous self-control in dealing with potential clients. Either they charge outrageous fees, eliminating many possible clients; they only consult 1 day a week; or they only accept clients located in idyllic settings such as Hawaii, Florida, or southern California.

On occasion they will work in Arizona in the winter or in Europe during the spring. Other scholars accept only contracts that allow them to perform research or deal with unique issues in their field. In turn, this often places them in the position of being the only one in their field with adequate research opportunities to address the Gordian Knot that seduces them.

In any of the above scenarios, so long as you constantly market yourself and let people know you do consult but are booked solid, for whatever reason, you will continue to get work. Often, scholars who make themselves scarce end up getting more business than ever based on the classic concept of exclusivity. It's a reverse psychology marketing ploy!

The other solution to this conundrum, of course, is to leave academe and consult full-time, building a new consulting firm in the marketplace. This is a monumental step, especially when many teaching slots are disappearing as a result of difficult economic conditions. It is easy to leave teaching. It may be difficult to return. However, many consulting scholars have done so with enormous personal, financial, and academic success, while providing us with a rich variety of alternatives and role models. Some examples follow:

MAC (Management Analysis Center). MAC is the classic success story of a group of Harvard Business School professors who got together and listed the support of colleagues at other leading business schools around the country. A few years ago, MAC had grown to more than $50 million a year in billings. It merged with PRC (Planning Research Corporation). A few years ago both were acquired by SOGETI, a large French firm similar to EDS. Most of the original founding partners of MAC today are small millionaires for their efforts.

The Portsmouth Group. Steve Jenks and several colleagues, all of whom were organizational behavior (OB) specialists in northeastern schools, formed a tribe of consultants that swarms to any client, able to work on any project larger than any individual can handle. The success of this approach has been phenomenal. Jenks states that his key to success is no more than 12 people in the tribe. Over the years, he has assisted more than 10 people start other similar tribes around the country. There is a growing list of people who want to join the tribe or start new tribes with Jenks.

Delta Group. David Nadler was teaching at Columbia in the OB field when he formed his own firm in New York. Although he continues close affiliations with his former colleagues on the Columbia faculty, the Delta Group has taken on ever-larger projects and now consults almost exclusively to Fortune 100 clients. Much of the firm's success has been due to Nadler's continued research, publications in leading journals, and the sophisticated marketing materials and white papers he produces for clients. Though he may not be teaching on a regular basis, Nadler is every bit the scholar he ever was in academia. He just makes a great deal more money doing it!

K-T and DDI. Ed Kepner and Ben Tregoe were researchers at the Rand Corporation in the early 1950s working on decision-making processes. They came across some models they believed were important. Rand Corp. wasn't interested. Kepner and Tregoe left, pursued their research, and developed some highly proprietary processes to help line managers make better decisions. They sold their processes to Fortune 100 companies in a series of midlevel managerial seminars. They also had the foresight to open offices in Europe and Asia in the early 1960s and were among the first U.S. consulting firms to move abroad before the age of globalization. The rest is history. By the 1980s, the firm had grown to be a $40-million-a-year training and development (T&D) firm that was acquired by the insurance firm of USF&G in Baltimore.

Development Dimensions International (DDI) is a K-T-like T&D firm in Pittsburgh, founded by Bill Byham, a researcher and scholar in the field of managerial assessment. He teamed up with Jim Robinson out of the University of Syracuse.

Together they have built a firm that provides training and development to Fortune 1,000 managers and executives using proprietary concepts and materials on an international scale. Many scholars associated with the T&D field believe that T&D internationally will grow to be a $4-billion market annually by the year 2001. The downside is that many consulting purists trash T&D firms like K-T and DDI, saying that once a company focuses on selling proprietary products with high profit margins, the exercise becomes one of "putting butts in seats," earning so much money per head off the training materials, rather than developing creative problem solving through the use of research and elegant solutions.

CEO. The Center for Effective Organization founded and managed by Ed Lawler at the University of Southern California is an example of a consulting organization under the tight control of a formal research center within a graduate school. Corporate sponsors are aggressively solicited for contributions and the consulting work that is performed is delivered at lower than market rates by very competent graduate students and researchers. The research that comes out of those efforts provides a rich environment of experimentation and discovery, financially supports the very bright people in the center, and has brought international recognition to the efforts of the center and its various research over the years.

All of these stories are about very successful academics who have leveraged their consulting skills and passions to become more than just part-time consulting scholars. There is no reason you cannot have a success similar to theirs if you have the same dedication and are willing to work the 16-hour days such independent ventures require.

Hire a Lawyer

Liability Avoidance. With more lawyers licensed to practice in southern California than there are members of the Screen

Actors Guild, it shouldn't be too difficult to find one to help you if you are teaching in that region of the country. What you want is someone who has experience helping small companies get started, incorporate, and register with the Secretary of State. "But, why do I need a corporate lawyer?" you ask. Good question.

Incorporation. Although I am not aware of any one of my consulting colleagues over the past 25 years who has been sued for malpractice by a client, it is important that you establish a corporate veil behind which you can protect your personal assets from the assets of your consulting enterprise. It is even difficult in this day and age to obtain professional "errors and omissions insurance" unless you manage a very large firm akin to one of the Big 6 accounting partnerships.

Tax Avoidance. With an incorporated business entity, most of the expenses related to business development, office equipment rental, and even leased automobiles can be deducted legitimately from your consulting revenues, and such revenues often are taxed at lower overall rates than your salary from the university. Furthermore, there are ways to move a broad range of personal expenses legitimately under the corporate tax umbrella so that, overall, your taxes can be reduced if you incorporate.

Liability Limitation. Even if you cannot find an insurance company that offers professional errors and omissions insurance coverage, recall from Business Administration 101 that the liability risks to a partnership or a sole proprietorship are far greater to you than if you incorporate your consulting activity. In the early 1990s, a number of very large damage suits have been decided against big six audit and consulting firms; individual partners are now facing personal financial ruin.

Flexibility. Perhaps the greatest benefit to incorporation is the flexibility it provides you in setting aside earnings toward your retirement, in offering partial ownership of the venture to the best and the brightest you want to recruit, and in allowing you the freedom to organize the ownership and the management of your enterprise in a variety of ways to support the uniqueness of your effort.

Protection. Overall, owning a small professional corporation is about the best business format you can have. There are any number of regulations, both state and federal, that limit and protect your liability and support your viability. As a small business with under 50 employees, there is no need to comply with EEO-Affirmative Action regulations or a host of other challenges faced by larger enterprises. If you develop any proprietary training materials, marketing brochures, or conceptual models, you will need to incorporate them under patent or copyright laws, and your lawyer should be able to help you do so.

Find a Good CPA

You might ask, "I've never needed a CPA before, why do I suddenly need one now?" Good question.

Tax Management. I was fortunate early in my incorporation to find "Mandrake the Magician," a very entrepreneurial and proactive CPA from Notre Dame. He helped me for almost 20 years and saved me untold amounts in taxes legitimately. Although you may never know Mandrake, a good, bright local CPA with a thriving small business practice can help you to earn and save tens of thousands of dollars every year if your consulting activity becomes significant. Even if you remain a part-time consulting scholar, a good CPA can help to reduce your tax liability.

Expense Maximization. The more you consult, the more you will want to make your practice a state-of-the-art effort with cellular telephones, fax machines, an account with Federal Express, and a computer capable of driving NASA programs. A new SAAB or BMW is a nice touch for your psyche, too. How you handle and expense such costs can make a big difference in what you can afford or accomplish.

Payroll Taxes and Withholding. Although you may not have very grand fantasies around your consulting efforts, you will need someone to handle your quarterly filings. Unlike your salary from the university, your consulting revenues must be filed separately each quarter and you must pay taxes based on projected earnings. Furthermore, the minute you engage someone else to do anything, be it clean up the office, or work with you as a consultant, you must administer their payroll and taxes monthly under tremendous penalties if you forget or do it wrong! Let your CPA worry about these things for you. For a small additional monthly fee, most good CPAs have administrative services to take care of such things for small businesses.

Fringe Benefits. As a small business, you well may qualify for group health and life insurance, IRAs, and other pension-related programs for yourself and your key people. You will need a well-read and well-trained CPA to maximize these benefits for you and your organization.

Financing. One consulting project leads to another. Adding one MBA to the staff leads to a gaggle of graduate students on the payroll. Soon, your receivables are in six figures but your bank account isn't, and you have to approach your bankers about some interim financing. This is only possible if you have a solid set of books, maintained by a CPA known to the community, who can answer any questions the bankers may have, and who can attest to the stability of your practice and the success of your business development efforts.

Cultivate a Banker

Although you may never have needed a banker in your career before, other than someone to finance your mortgage, now that you are running a business, you need a banker.

To Maximize Earnings. As your little practice grows and succeeds, you will find yourself with excess cash before you realize it. And, while it is a good rule of thumb to keep at least 3 months' operating expenses in a cash account, as a corporation, there are various investments available to you, such as *bankers acceptances,* that yield higher rates than what you may experience from your personal savings account or a money market account.

To Develop a Safety Net. As you have greater and greater amounts of receivables, you will find ever greater stress on your cash flow. At some time you will need someone to advance you enough for your payroll or other expenses, even if it is only for a few weeks.

To Obtain Leverage. You may want $10,000 to finance a new computer or $15,000 for new furnishings or $25,000 for a new company car. All such credit is directly proportionate to how well your banker knows and understands the details of your practice and your creditworthiness as an entrepreneur.

To Provide Advice. The stronger your personal relationship to your banker, the more help he or she can be, informing you of the bank's current lending posture, advising you on how to dress up your financial reports, or sharing with you his or her opinion of the local economy. Also, a banker with your interests in mind can be a resource for endless leads to troubled companies in need of consultants and bank customers whose payments are slowing.

As a Potential Client. Most banks I have dealt with are poorly managed organizations in need of organizational and marketing support. If you have the right relationship with your banker, over time, you may find a new client for yourself.

All this means that it is critical for you to shop around to find a banker interested in your business and what you do. Ideally, if it is a previous student who knew you as a professor or teacher, at least you have instant credibility. But, you want more than a typical neighborhood branch manager. You want to find a bank that is committed in its lending to small businesses, and a banker who is willing to listen and understand what it is you do and how you do it. The relationship becomes a partnership, with you seeking to find as many ways to help the bank as the bank can help you. You will know it has been a successful effort when the first time you ask for some credit it is forthcoming with a minimum of fuss. It really is just one more sale you have to make in life!

So find a banker about your own age, in a bank interested in helping smaller businesses, help them to understand your business as if they were a prospect for a consulting project. Open personal accounts at the bank, and your company accounts there as well. And start building a long-term relationship. If you truly are successful building a firm, you will need the banking connection to swing the $500,000 loan for your new corporate headquarters in the refurbished turn-of-the-century 15-room Victorian house!

Setting Up an Office

On a far smaller scale, when should you get an office apart from your spare bedroom or your office at the university? The answer is different for each of us. Some of the deciding factors follow:

Leverage. As long as you continue to teach full-time you should leverage the amenities of your departmental administration: photocopies, supplies, library facilities, telephone answering and message services, the use of research assistants, student gofers, and so forth.

Balance. Once your consulting activities begin to take more and more of your time, and you begin to find yourself in conflict with the restrictions on consulting as expressed by your college or university policies, you need to move your activities to your residence. A spare bedroom or a corner of the family room often work for most of us. However, there are two important points to make here. First, whatever part of your home you set apart for your consulting effort should be consistent and unique (for tax purposes), and second, wherever you establish your office in your home should be a quiet place where you can concentrate and your family will leave you in peace. You should not tolerate a situation in which a client calls you only to hear a baby crying or a dog barking in the background.

Transition. When your consulting begins to dominate your professional work and time, and you find you cannot support your clients' needs entirely on your own, nor can your department at school support your own administrative support needs, it is time to consider a separate office facility. In many major metropolitan areas there are executive office suites available on monthly rental, which also provide telephone answering and clerical support facilities in very prestigious business addresses. Many young lawyers and other new entrepreneurs use such facilities. Some are very well managed and are worth the expense.

The Early Years. At the same time, there are some considerations as you establish your new consulting enterprise. First, you do not want to be seen changing your address and phone numbers every 3 to 6 months. Your clients will not get a solid impression of your practice.

Second, every time you move or change phone numbers, you face the additional expense of new stationery and calling cards, and even marketing materials. Perhaps, the best advice is to take on the burden of a separate office space when: your cash flow can support it; you find you must hire additional personnel and they deserve a decent and comfortable, professional work setting; and you know you will be leaving academe.

Be Practical. Too many new consultants flatter themselves and their egos by taking on expensive space for purely ego-driven reasons. Unless your clients are coming to visit you, you have no need for posh offices and their related costs. You do need to be in a space that affords the flexibility to expand as your practice grows, and a location that is easy for your staff to commute to. You may even consider locating in an industrial park near the airport if your practice requires a great deal of travel.

Other factors to take into consideration are the needs and egos of the staff you are attempting to recruit. As you hire ambitious, professional staff, your image to them is as important in the recruiting process as whatever image your office may project to potential clients. You need professional-looking areas, preferably in a newer building. Whatever you do, shop around. There are very few communities these days that do not have a glut of commercial office space, and if you shop effectively and make outrageous demands, you will be shocked at what you can accomplish. I am aware of a colleague who ended up with twice the space his organization needed in one of the best buildings in downtown Houston. Not only was the first year of the lease free but the landlord threw in four rooms full of luxury office furnishings that had been abandoned by a former tenant that failed financially. We all can't relocate to Houston, but this should serve as an example of what you can accomplish with some tough bargaining and a little patience.

Furthermore, you do not need to spend your first profits on $10,000 Baker desks or on new $2,500 designer filing cabinets. Whenever my partners and I opened a new facility, we found the local used furniture store and completely filled our needs for everything from the reception area to the library and lunch room with quality used pieces for only a few dollars. Remember to order just what you really need. You can always add additional pieces or cabinets later.

Hiring Others

One of the most profound dialogues I ever had with my daughter while she was a student at Boston University evolved around her and her then boyfriend wanting to visit the local pet shelter and adopt an abandoned kitten. What they had not considered was the fact that beyond the novelty of the first 3 months, they had a responsibility for as long as 10 years. What would they do with the kitten whenever they wanted to go on vacation? How would the vet's bills affect their limited personal budget? And how would they care for the cat when it was ill and they had classes or work responsibilities?

I use this example as parable for the awesome responsibilities you take on when you decide to hire someone to work with you in your consulting practice. This is just as true if you hire a young parent to be a secretary cum administrative assistant or if you hire a recently graduated MBA with a family and a mortgage to support. You cannot do these things lightly, so you do them rarely. I lost a wonderful partner, once, a Ph.D. with three master's degrees. He loved consulting and the challenge of performing business development efforts; however, one morning he walked into the office, surveyed the long office bay housing 10 professional and 6 clerical people, and was shocked to realize that all these people and their families, perhaps 50 people in all, were dependent on him and me to bring new business in regularly to maintain the success of the firm. Suddenly, what started out as fun and a way to make more money than he could in teaching and research wasn't fun any more.

Next to having your first child, hiring your first full-time employee is an awesome responsibility. The best way to ensure that it is a successful hire is to be certain the work exists not for one more person, but for at least two. Not only does this ensure your new hire will be earning his or her keep, but also it provides you with some leeway should business slow down —you won't be forced to let your new hire go. Most consulting firms I have managed or been associated with would not hire a new secretary unless consistently for several months there was additional work for two or three staff members, and they would not begin interviewing possible new consultants unless the partners felt they were short two or three consultants.

The Organization of It All

What all this concentrates out to is a business that must be planned and managed very carefully. *Control* is a major factor. Not control over your people as much as control over the internal process and the administration of everyone's time. One of the most important employees you can and should hire early on in your organization is an office manager or *practice administrator*. This is the very bright, $40,000-a-year individual who will keep you organized and everyone else in the process. This administrator should not be a martinet as much as a very pleasant helper who reminds everyone that time and expense reports are due, who makes sure the invoices are correct and go out to clients on schedule, who sees that the bills get paid, and who checks that the office staff is organized and coordinated to address crash projects at the last minute, and who makes sure that the supply cabinet and the icebox remain full. You need a certain critical mass of business before you can afford someone like this, but once

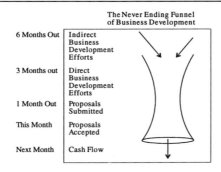

Figure 6.1. The Never-Ending Funnel of Business Development

that level of activity is achieved, you will be hard pressed to do without him or her.

Primarily, too, you need to maintain control over the business development process. Starting 6 months beforehand with the impact of indirect business development efforts and culminating in the proposals requested by prospects this month, a never-ending process is set in motion. And the larger the practice, the greater the ebb and flow through the funnel as shown in Figure 6.1.

To manage such a process successfully, you must set in motion procedures that carefully develop the detailed work plans for each proposal, projecting exactly how many hours of professional and staff time will be generated by the project on a cumulative basis. By forecasting 2 to 3 months ahead, you can project that some 1,800 person-hours are needed in November if all current proposals outstanding are approved and become contracts. In a given month 1,800 hours equals 10 full-time professional staff members. How will you handle it if you only have six or eight people available? Time to start lining up part-timers and networking with other firms for peoples' time 2 months out! Figure 6.2 is an example of a project planning sheet. Figure 6.3 shows a professional time

DEWEY, CHEETUM & HOWE

Project Planning Form

CLIENT: _____   PROJECT: _____

ACCT. MGR.: _____   DATE: _____

CONSULTANT	TASK	HOURS	RATE	EST. FEES

TOTALS

Plus RELATED
ESTIMATED EXPENSES @ 20% of Fees

TOTAL TO BE PROPOSED:

ANTICIPATED BILLING:

					Totals
Month					
Amount					

Figure 6.2. A Worksheet for Project Planning

management sheet that combines all your project planning sheets together to forecast your firm's work load.

Furthermore, administrative procedures must be in place that actually account for the professional and staff hours devoted to each project so that the time actually expended is tracked against the hours for which there is a client budget. Figure 6.4 is a time sheet all employees must complete each week. It is not to check up on them but to account for their

DEWEY, CHEETUM & HOWE
Time Management Form
For the month of _____

Project			Total Hours**

Total Hours
Required Per Staff
**Total project hours should relate back to the project planning worksheet.

Figure 6.3. A Sample Time Management Form

time so it can be billed out to generate the funds for their paycheck! When the need for this information is explained in those terms, few employees ever complain.

But just as each proposal is costed out in terms of staff time, so must everyone on the payroll be accountable as to how he or she uses the hours available. When the hours are not chargeable to a client project, they are a direct cost factor for you. If staff members have nothing to do, they should be out performing business development or somehow improving their technical skills. Just think about the cost of holding a meeting in your office with two bright staff members. Your

DEWEY, CHEETUM & HOWE

Time Sheet

For the week ending: _____

Client Project	Mon.	Tues.	Wed.	Thurs.	Fri.	Sat.	Sun.
Total Hours Chargeable							
Travel							
Professional Development							
Vacation or Holiday							
Business Development							
Illness							
Total Non-Chargeable							

Figure 6.4. A Sample Time Sheet

"burn" rate is $250 an hour and theirs may be $150 each. This equals $550 for a 1-hour meeting. If it is not billable to a client, it comes straight out of your pocket! Such is the burden of being the managing principal!

Another form that is a helpful tool for your new and expanding practice is a proposal work plan. Figure 6.5 shows what such a plan would look like for scoping out a strategic planning project with a community bank. It is merely a scratch

Dewey, Cheetum & Howe
Proposal Work Plan
For: Not for Nuthin National Bank (NNNB)
Project: Strategic Planning Retreat
Date: May 5
Client Manager: George Howe

Step	Week	Procedure	Staff	Days	Location
1	I	Gather all historical documentation	1C	0.5	Client (first visit)
2	I	Interview executive committee members (6)	1C	2.0	Client
3	I	Interview all senior VPs and dept. heads (10)	1C	2.0	Client
4	II	Analyze all financial and lending data collected and all board minutes for the last 3 years	2R	4.0	Office
5	II	Develop any financially based issues or hypotheses from data review	2R	2.0	Office
6	II	Meet to review financial and interview data, seek to develop initial strategic hypotheses	2C/2R	2.0	Office
7	II	Review all marketing and competitive data collected, including regional industry comparative data	2R	2.0	Office
8	III	Draft initial report on basic strategic issues and hypotheses	1C/1A	2.0	Office
9	III	Develop strategic questionnaire	1C/1A	2.0	Office
10	III	Initial hypotheses report and questionnaire reviewed by a principal (QC)	1P	0.5	Office
11	IV	Review initial strategic issues and strategic questionnaire with executive committee	1C	1.0	Client (second visit)

Figure 6.5. A Sample Proposal Work Plan

Step	Week	Procedure	Staff	Days	Location
12	IV	Meet with 11 managers to announce and explain strategic questionnaire and answer questions	1C	0.5	Client
13	IV	Meet with chairman to set dates and location for strategic retreat	1C	0.5	Client
14	V	Begin analysis of returned questionnaires	2R/1A	7.0	Office
15	VI	Create master question-naire with consensus answers for retreat Delphi exercise	1C/1A	2.0	Office
16	VI	Meet to review responses against early hypotheses	1P/2C/ 2R	4.0	Office
17	VI	Modify hypotheses and determine if secon-dary interviews are necessary—send letter to chairman	1C/1A	1.0	Office
18	VII	Meet to stage secondary interviews	1C	2.0	Client (third visit)
19	VII	Meet with executive committee to answer any final questions before retreat	1C	0.5	Client
20	VII	Meet internally to review and plan retreat agenda	1P/2C	2.0	Office
21	VIII	Manage and facilitate 2-day strategic retreat	1P/2C	6.0	Client (fourth visit)
22	IX	Develop and condense retreat notes, address outstanding issues, and provide work assignments to members of management	2C/2A	4.0	Office
23	IX	Develop cover letter to client with materials and work assignments	1C/1A	1.0	Office
24	X	Visit client to review issues and coach on assignments made	2C	1.0	Client (fifth visit)

Figure 6.5. Continued

Step	Week	Procedure	Staff	Days	Location
25	X	Meet with executive committee to plan and organize second retreat	2C	1.0	Client (sixth visit)
26	XI	Manage and facilitate second 2-day retreat	1P/2C	6.0	Client (seventh visit)
27	XI	Work up final strategic position paper for client together with major assignments and key dates	2C/2A	4.0	Office
28	XII	Deliver final notes and position paper and meet with chairman to sell add-on work	1P/2C	3.0	Client (eighth visit)

SUMMARY

10 days of Principal	@ $3,000/day	$30,000
41 days of Consultants	@ $1,500/day	$61,500
16 days of Researchers	@ $800/day	$12,800
15 days of Admin. Staff	@ $400/day	$6,000
Total Fees to Propose		$110,300

Plus:

Retreat supplies, flip charts, reading assignments, development of questionnaires, postage, envelopes, etc. @ $500 per Retreat	$1,000
Seven trips to client including airfare, two hotel nights, rental cars, and meals @ $2,000 per trip	$14,000
Overhead assigned @ 10% of professional fees	$11,000
Total Related Expenses:	$26,000

APPROVED: _____

pad for you to think through how you will perform a particular job and what it will cost versus what you decide to bid.

Figure 6.6 is an expense form. I have looked at expense forms for more than 25 years, constantly searching for something better. I haven't found it anymore than I ever found Truth. A

DEWEY, CHEETUM & HOWE

Expense Report

For the week ending: _____

Client Project	Mon.	Tues.	Wed.	Thurs.	Fri.	Sat.	Sun.
Total Hours Chargeable							
Travel							
Hotel and Lodgings							
Meals and Refreshments							
Business Development							
Entertainment							
Telephone, fax, & express delivery							
Miscellaneous							
Total Client Chargeable							

Figure 6.6. Sample Expense Report Form

good expense form helps you charge back your costs connected with a project to clients and account for business development and other operating expenses. A standard policy in your firm should be that no one gets paid unless he or she has turned in a time sheet and an expense report for the previous period. Even if a staff member didn't have one billable hour, these data are what *you* need to manage *your* company!

Conclusion

This chapter has been a sobering discourse. What started out as an intellectually intriguing exercise has become an all-consuming responsibility. That's no fun! Which goes to emphasize that unless you really enjoy managing all these issues and the challenge of the responsibilities they generate and unless your psyche requires the sense of accomplishment that accompanies building an organization such as I have described, you probably don't want to leave academe for a full-time consulting career. Let's say you have made that decision, you still may be silently asking me, "Okay, okay, when can I have the office on Park Avenue with the mahogany Baker furniture, the British receptionist, and the research assistant from Radcliffe?" The answer is maybe never!

Be realistic. You have started a professional services practice and have hired some very competent young people. They should look forward to commuting to their jobs each day because it is challenging and fun. This also implies that even though you found the deal of the century on your lease and the furnishings, you still want to have a comfortable, light, airy, spacious set of digs. I always included a generously equipped kitchen with a full-size refrigerator, microwave oven, dish washer, and a complete set of upscale china from Sears. This encourages people to bring their lunch with them and maybe even dinner so that they'll stay late on their own initiative. Staff members may even send out for pizza or Chinese! There were always plenty of soft drinks and the lunch room tended to be a place for informal meetings and discussions about client issues and work and project planning. My partners and I also felt strongly about having a professional library on the premises, similar to what can be found in a good law firm. Back issues of the *Harvard Business Review, The California*

Management Review, and *The Sloan Management Review,* together with a pooled library of industry data, business books, and textbooks, organized by field of study, usually came together to provide the staff with a rich source of reading and research whatever the problems of the day. Finally, having recruited these very special people, my partners and I believed we could not spend much on our own amenities before we had at least 3 months' cash flow in the savings account to support everyone during a slow period when no new business was coming in. That meant $100,000 cash in a savings account for them, not us. So much for the Baker furniture!

7 | The Strategic Perspective

The Criticality of Focus

With so many opportunities to consult and so many consultants already in the marketplace, the third most important perspective you must develop is that of defining in some specificity just what kind of a practice you want to create. This is the strategic perspective. The major axes of the basic model are the market and the method, that is, is the expertise you can offer industry specific, discipline specific, or field specific? And which of the many styles of consulting best suits your sense of values and abilities? This chapter explores different strategic alternatives and evaluates the implications of the practice strategy you ultimately develop. The key reasons for developing a clear practice strategy include the following:

Market Identification. If you aren't sure what it is you do, how can the marketplace know? When all is said and done, you haven't built a consulting practice until you have clients. Clients, in turn, have very specific needs and issues to discuss when hiring a consultant. So where does your expertise lie? Are you a specialist with particular knowledge about a specific industry, such as financial services or health care? How about a geographic region such as the Northeast or the Pacific Rim? Or a particular professional discipline, from family counseling and psychology to organization and work design? Or is your expertise research based in your field of science: inorganic chemistry, astrophysics, or particle wave analysis? Each of these choices helps to clarify who you are and what you provide in the way of expertise to the marketplace.

Competitive Advantage. Specifying the focus of your practice also creates your *competitive posture* in the marketplace. What specifically do you bring to your industry or discipline that others do not or cannot provide? Have you been performing family counseling for more than 20 years or have you spent the past 15 years performing research about compensation in the mining industry? Perhaps you have been called as an expert witness in more than a dozen art fraud trials? What can you provide to clients that no other person or firm can provide? A part of that answer may be in the fact that you offer those services in a specific market area, say the Boston-Hartford corridor or throughout the Midwest.

Practice Guidelines. In defining these specifics, you also are defining where you will work and how large a marketplace exists for you, locally, nationally, or internationally. This tends to affect how hard you intend to work, that is, how much time each month you will devote to your consulting practice, how many days you will make available for marketing your services, and as a result, who your competitors may be. If you are a specialist in family counseling and you really do not enjoy traveling outside the Chicago area, then you have defined the boundaries of your market and who your competitors are. If you are a specialist in strategic planning in, say, commercial banking, then the opportunity exists for you to provide those services to any of the more than 10,000 banks in this country, and your competitors will range from the local two-man partnership of retired bankers around the corner, to half the economics department in your university, to all of the Big 6 accounting firms, plus McKinsey & Company and Booz, Allen. Lots of luck!

Types of Consulting Practices

Having determined the general scope of what you want to do (and by definition, what you will not do), the next major decision point is the style of practice you will develop. There are many different styles for a consulting practice, and each has its own focus and flavor.

Content Versus Process. This is one of the fundamental divisions in the consulting profession. *Content* consultants tend to leverage off their personal expertise and unique knowledge to tell the client what the problem is and what, specifically, should be done about it. In the extreme, say in crisis management or business turnaround projects, this can take on the role of surrogate management. Content consulting goes back to the turn of the century when Frederick Taylor went so far as to design 20 different kinds of coal shovels to improve a client's productivity. Often this style of direct, take-charge assistance is just what the client needs, especially if the client organization is small, management's experience is limited, and the organization cannot afford the level of expertise internally that is needed to resolve the issues in question.

Process consultants take a different view (see Schein, 1969). They believe that the greatest service they can provide a client organization is *discovery*. Rather than tell the client what is wrong, process consultants tend to focus their energies on helping the client to surface and understand the problem, and most important, to take ownership of the problem. They, then, work with the client to help develop solutions and to design and manage the change process that must take place. However, process consultants tend to let the client take authorship for the decisions to improve the situation. In this way, process consultants believe that the learning that occurs within the client's organization will stick. They have seen—especially in larger, more sophisticated enterprises—that when a content consultant leaves, things tend to revert to their earlier state. In other words, the problem was the consultant's problem; the solution or the plan, the consultant's plan; and the moment something doesn't quite work out, it is, naturally, the consultant's fault! In the end, many clients tend to blame consultants for the hangover or believe that the money they spent on content consultants was not well spent. Often process consultants will be so indirect that they will limit their relationship with clients merely to asking questions in an almost Freudian scenario: "Where does it hurt? Why do you believe that? On what facts do you base your conclusions? What might be a solution? What would your organization think about that?" Process consultation tends to be more effective for larger organizations that have well-trained and well-educated managers and a strong sense of teamwork.

Generalist Versus Specialist. Generalists tend to take a holistic approach to helping clients. In the field of business, a generalist management consultant might work with senior management and the board to help develop strategy, with marketing to design market research, with personnel to review fringe benefits, and with operations to improve quality in the product development area. And if key expertise is lacking in the organization, this intrepid consultant might even offer to perform the executive search work required to find and recruit a new chief financial officer. Such generalists believe that their unique insight to and understanding of the client organization, coupled with their years of experience in general management, gives them the ability to act as a spare pair of hands in the board room and on the shop floor. They often are considered by the client to be a part of the management team and are asked to get involved wherever they believe they can be helpful. Frequently, this level of general counsel works best with smaller, newer businesses. There is no possible way for a generalist to work in all areas of an organization as huge as, say, General Electric, ITT, or IBM. However, such general counsel is exactly what is provided by a number of business school professors working in a shadow management role. They are the one person the business owner or managers can talk openly with, and they have the personal credibility to provide a level of comfort that senior management desperately needs.

Specialists tend to focus their work with clients on their singular area of expertise—they try to do one thing very, very well. Many successful consulting practices are strategically positioned in this fashion. Whether it is training and development, organization and job design, strategic planning, operations management, tax and accounting systems, management succession planning in family-owned and -managed businesses, or information systems and software development, specialists believe that no matter what the industry, its competitive issues are so complex in this day and age that their practice can exist only by providing a level of expertise greater than that any client can develop internally. Specialists believe that the generalists overstep prudent levels of counsel and never work long enough in any one discipline to understand it adequately to be truly competitive in the counsel they do provide.

Custom Versus Package. A third major strategic perspective to be determined in establishing your consulting practice is the extent to which you want to treat each client's need as unique. *Custom* consultants do just that. They believe that no matter how many health care organizations engage you to design their management information systems, and in spite of the fact that there is a body of information required of every health care facility to manage it effectively, every single client organization is unique and the solutions provided need to be custom designed.

Package consultants are strongly in opposition to this strategy. A package consultant will work very hard to develop a generic approach to particular client needs (especially in training and development) and to design an effective solution (usually in the form of a program or seminar that can be delivered to various levels in the client's organization). These consultants will basically deliver the same solution to similar problems, regardless of the client's possibly unique needs. The package consultant will tell you that it is wasteful of a client's resources to custom design every solution when certain basic approaches tend to work 95% of the time. What the package consultant won't reveal is that the first client underwrote the entire cost of the program's development and every solution sold after that is "pure gravy." As long as the solution doesn't get stale, it's one of the most lucrative forms of consulting. Custom consultants will retort that this is not consulting but an exercise of "putting butts in seats."

Diagnostic Versus Implementation. Another dichotomy for conceptualizing your practice is that of the diagnostic versus the implementation consultant. *Diagnostic* practices, for the most part, use highly analytical MBA types boring past symptoms to discover the root causes of an organization's problems. They develop very powerful audiovisual presentations of their findings and may, on occasion, offer possible solutions, but their relationship with their clients stops there. For a wide range of reasons (from size of the projects to skills required of the staff, to malpractice liability, to hourly billing rates), diagnostic groups do not get involved with solutions or implementing needed change.

Implementation specialists thrive on being agents of change. They recognize that most managers are competent to operate their companies but focus on command and control of the status quo. As a result, they are not facile at managing change or the change process. Therefore, implementation specialists work with clients to discover the issues, often through process consultation, and then focus their energies on helping the client with the change process. They implement solutions—fearlessly.

Each of these biases is client, problem, and solution specific. The arguments that abound over which is the "correct" way to approach a particular client or issue are endless. What is important to you is where within all these perspectives do you feel most comfortable and can you be most productive for your clients? Whatever you come up with in response is the correct answer!

Jump In and Get Wet

This chapter and the two preceding it are meant to help you position yourself, to help you state what kind of consultant you are and what you do—and what you do not do. But to reap the rewards, you must let people know. Most initial consulting leads for scholars come through their department chair or the dean's office, a few come via your college's public relations organization and sometimes even the alumni association. Develop a one-page flier and get it out to everyone. Grant an interview to the alumni news organ, for example.

Institutions such as the University of Southern California and the University of Western Ontario in Canada have MBA elective programs devoted to teaching consulting skills and techniques and to developing case studies for teaching consulting skills in the classroom. If your schedule permits, enroll in one. Dozens of other universities around the world use standard texts in their programs built around the industry and consulting principles. The National Academy of Management has an entire division (Management Consultancy) devoted to the scholarly study of consulting skills and processes. It encourages closer ties in action research between consulting academics and management consulting firms. There are numerous opportunities for scholars to network with professional consultants and consulting organizations, and to become associated with them on a formal basis as an alternative to managing a solo practice. There are also numerous individuals such as Carl Sloane, John Hartshorne, and Jim Kennedy, who have devoted their time tirelessly to help move the industry closer to professional status.

Finally, there is the Institute of Management Consultants.[1] The IMC is a private professional association for approximately 2,250 independent consultants, consulting scholars, and small firms. It provides basic training in consulting and marketing skills through seminars held around the country. It has numerous regional chapters in major cities and confers the designation Certified Management Consultant (CMC) on qualifying members. The IMC has a code of conduct and ethics and is supported by numerous industry leaders. It also has its own journal, *The Journal of Management Consulting,* which is published quarterly. Some larger accounting firms such as the Management Services Division of Deloitte, Touche insist that all of their consultants meet the qualifications and become confirmed CMCs. The IMC has a nonvoting member on the executive committee of the Management Consultancy Division of the Academy of Management and provides financial support to the division's best paper award each year.

Perhaps the best way to learn and grow in your work as a consulting scholar is to develop your own network of peers around the country or in your chosen industry or field, as per the model of the Portsmouth Group (see pp. 93-94 of this book). Few consultants really work alone, and most meaningful consulting assignments require a partnership of some kind, if not with a local firm, then with a colleague. Talk to your peers, see who is publishing articles in your industry's journals and who is speaking on the conference circuit. Get to know them, let them know you are interested in consulting, and become a part of their network. And always benchmark your fees to the marketplace!

Note

1. The address for the IMC is 521 Fifth Avenue, 35th floor, New York, NY 10175.

8 | The Heuristic Perspective

As I get up and walk around the computer one more time, I feel that I have said just about all that I have to say on this subject. However, there are some loose ends that I will attempt to organize in some rational fashion to end our discourse. Probably this should include looping your consulting activities back to the classroom, the practicality of living as a full-time consultant, and the ethics of the profession.

Looping Back to the Classroom

One of the most straightforward links between your consulting and the classroom can be the design and development of a graduate program around consultative skills. Each of the attributes discussed earlier in the book that lead to effective consulting are the same attributes required to be a successful change agent and diagnostician within a large organization today. And these skills are being regarded ever more highly. Teaching graduate students, be their concentration in business administration, organization and work design, communications, or psychology, is a most rewarding activity. To help them prepare to be effective at planning and managing change in an ever-changing paradigm is a critical need in business school curricula. It is one of the abilities many of the newly designed MBA programs will include.

Greiner and I developed a program at USC in the late 1970s that continues to this day and has been a role model for a number of similar programs throughout the country. The course is composed of lectures around our text, *Consulting to Management*. We also invited a broad range of leading consultants from the Los Angeles region whom we had screened over time as effective speakers. One of the very real problems you will face with consultants as guest lecturers is that because it is such a lonely avocation consultants tend to toot their own horns. This is not at all helpful to the students. They are not as much interested in what a person has achieved as *how* they achieved it. Graduate students are eager for the craft skills and secrets, not the bravura.

A second very successful source of guest lecturers in the program were former students who had graduated and joined local consulting firms in the previous 5 years. They would come and talk about their transition from line manager to consultant and how they had applied the skills learned in the course to real consulting situations. Many of these former students became mainstays to the program.

Another key point of the program's success was a loose approach to class schedules. The syllabus required a project that teams of three to four students had to market to a nonpaying client, and we left the students a great deal of class time to work on their projects. However, many of the skills that must be taught can only be done so in extended laboratory periods of 4 to 6 hours rather than in a short, 90-minute class during the week. Therefore, we staged three all-day Saturday labs during the semester to discuss and study cases about hypothesis development, skills required to enter a foreign culture, how to make effective oral presentations to clients, how to enroll clients, and so on.

Many of our colleagues debated strongly with us over whether or not students should be allowed to market consultative skills to nonpaying clients. It seems the greatest concern was one of liability for the college and possible risk to our credentials. Neither Greiner nor I ever had trepidations about this, because most of our students were older, mature, and had several years' experience working for major employers around the Los Angeles basin. The hard part was helping them find a client willing to let them in on the company's problems or become privy to the outrageous excesses of the owner-manager of the business. At Western Ontario in Canada, MBAs enroll in a two-semester program and are paid a stipend from federal Canadian funds for all the time they spend working on client accounts in their second-year efforts as fledgling consultants. Were that we could establish such apprenticeships here!

Research

If research is your first love, your consulting efforts can open up a wide spectrum of opportunities. As I mentioned earlier, designing solid research around client industry and market issues or issues as they are perceived by customers and markets offers marvelous opportunities. Again, you don't have to be an expert in your client's industry to provide the organization with your research skills. As Delbecq relates, what you develop as a project can lead to very real new knowledge for your client's industry and your field, while you leverage the work off what you know best as scholar. Furthermore, your writings can address the applicability of the research results to your client's industry or business.

Client-based research can cover the spectrum from customer attitudes to focus group studies, whereas industry and competitive-based studies can leverage off knowledge needed to penetrate new markets or meet unfulfilled customer needs, the applicability of new technologies to the client's industry, or a wealth of other, allied studies.

Oops, I Almost Forgot!

Consulting is hard work. One of the first things you may discover as you begin your consulting efforts is that consulting is very hard work. You travel a great deal whether you intend to or not. You work long hours to meet commitments made in proposals and as you become involved in your client's problems. Add in your regular teaching schedule; counseling your students; developing case materials, research studies, and new articles and you can burn out quickly if you are not careful.

Some of the things that I learned over the years to extend my own longevity include the following:

Travel Well. If you have to be on the road a lot, pace yourself. Find a good travel agent who will work for you to develop a manageable schedule, with realistic time between flights, rental cars waiting for you, and corporate rates at first-class hotels. This is not to suggest that you should go first class at the client's expense, but if you are working for a company, you should travel as well as any of their senior executives. The concept held by some clients that as a vendor you should stay in $30-a-night motels and limit the cost of your meals to $30 a day communicates that you are not perceived as a professional, engaged to resolve the client's critical issues.

Manage Your Time. Don't work more than 12 hours a day with any consistency. If you are to be effective for a client you need your rest and you need to reflect on the issues and solutions. When clients ask you to be in six different cities in five days, smile, but reschedule yourself. You cannot do quality analysis or insightful problem-resolution work when you are in a state of exhaustion. Try and keep some of each weekend for yourself. Although Monday through Wednesday classes allow you to consult Thursday through Saturday, Sunday should be a day of rest at home with family.

Exercise Regularly. There are few first-class hotels today that do not have spas or workout rooms with all the equipment you need to maintain your fitness program. It may be much more practical to spend a half hour on a treadmill in the hotel than to try to jog through the local park replete with muggers. Also, I have found that working out regularly provides an energy level that allows you to tolerate the long hours better than when you pursue a sedentary life.

Eat Smart. But eat well. Many people make the mistake when traveling on the client's expense account to eat steak and drink expensive wine. This is as bad as you can be to yourself. Good hotels provide a great opportunity to eat really luxurious salads of the kind that are too much trouble to make for yourself at home. I use traveling as an excuse to eat lots of fish. But, although I enjoy a glass of good wine, I restrict my alcoholic intake when on the road to ensure that I have a clear head in the morning and to maintain my stamina while flying around the country. Living well and extending your longevity is really just a matter of common sense.

Learn to Say No. This is the most difficult thing to do as a consultant and scholar. Everyone wants a piece of your life, from your family to your department chair, to your clients, to your colleagues, to your graduate students and research assistants. You cannot meet all of their needs and your own, too. To try is suicidal. Decline the trip you don't really need to make and the luncheon you really don't need to attend; get people, including clients, to meet on your schedule, but do so politely. And decline to bid on that piece of work that will bankrupt your schedule!

Invest in Technology. The costs of technology, a fast computer, extra RAM, a good laser printer, and a fax machine all are coming down weekly. There is no excuse not to spend a few thousand dollars of your first hard-earned consulting fees on these amenities of business life. They allow you to be highly productive and competitive even with much larger firms. Furthermore, your presentations, overheads, graphics, and slides communicate that you manage a serious consulting practice not something on the side in your spare time. This is very important in developing your professional image and in gaining new clients.

A Personal Bias

At this stage in my career, I am a hard-nosed Apple Macintosh freak. I bought one of the first MacPlus machines at a computer fair at USC in 1985 and have never looked back. What has been most rewarding over the years are the various software packages that have been developed for Apple systems. The ones I use most frequently to help me in my consulting work include the following seven:

❶ *MacWrite II*. This is one of the original Claris word-processing programs. I like it because it is fast, easy, and idiot proof. It allows me to develop a stationery outline for correspondence and reports and is easy to manage when writing longer proposals or client documents. It will handle an almost unlimited number of fonts and displays them as they will actually appear when you drag down on the menu. MacWrite II has a terrific dictionary and a very fast spell checker.

❷ *Microsoft Word 5.0*. This is more sophisticated than MacWrite II. It is a program for very long, complex documents such as the manuscript for this book. It has an excellent dictionary but a slower spell checker and doesn't allow you to see samples of the fonts you select. However, it has a built-in, simple graphics program for charts, diagrams, or forms development. And, like MacWrite II, it will transpose whatever you are doing into multiple columns for newsletters or brochures at the tap of a key.

❸ *Microsoft Excel 4.0*. This is a very powerful financial analysis tool. If you do a good deal of analysis off your client's annual reports and other financial and marketing data, you best set up your analytical format as a model. Excel documents merge beautifully with Word documents, too.

❹ *MacProject Pro.* This is the very latest program to design or manage complex projects. It really comes in handy when developing a sophisticated work plan and related proposals. The bigger the proposal and the more people involved, the easier MacProject makes it.

❺ *MORE.* MORE was originally just an outline program to draft client reports or presentations. However, you can break your key points down into what amounts to a slide or overheads and produce your materials on transparencies for a quick and easy presentation format. It also has a feature that permits you to design organizational charts of infinite complexity. Over the past 5 years, I have saved probably several months of my time using MORE.

❻ *JMP.* JMP is one of the most powerful statistical/analytical programs on the market today for either Apple or IBM clone products. It allows three-dimensional displays of your data in a multitude of ways and allows display rotation for visual presentations. This is one of the best research tools I know of, one that clients are able to understand and relate to.

❼ *Power Point.* This was one of the very first slide presentation programs, and I have used it for many years. It allows you to design and develop rather sophisticated slides or transparencies quickly for presentation to prospects or clients. Not many years ago, such work had to be taken out to graphics services and costed thousands of dollars. A few lengthy presentations developed on Power Point will save you the cost of your hardware!

With a fast Apple computer and these software packages, there is no reason why you cannot develop materials to present yourself and your work as truly professional. With a good fax machine, you can deliver it all instantly to Tokyo, and your career is launched.

A Darwinian Environment

Another perspective from heuristics is that consulting is a rapidly changing environment within which to compete. New knowledge transfer practices are springing up monthly, and unless you invest a good part of your time in reading all the important business school journals or the journals relevant to your field of endeavor, you will find yourself out of touch. In the experience transfer field, pragmatic managers with real shop-floor experience in managing change and teaching TQM principles are leaving industry to set up their own practices constantly. No matter how much reading or research you have performed as a scholar, it is very tough to take business away from someone who has worked with a Fortune 100 firm for 10 years managing change.

All of this competition translates into the concept that what worked yesterday is passé today and the one who was hot yesterday is old hat today. Clients face very difficult times and they must perceive that the fees they pay consultants are going to be high-yielding investments in the future rather than operational expenses today. Only the most well informed, heavily experienced in the very specific areas of client need will win and hold new clients in the future.

All of this is not meant to discourage you from consulting as much as it is meant to help you realize that the profession is serious business that can have enormous payoffs or disastrous results. Perhaps the best thing you can do for yourself is collaborate with others whenever possible. Try not to be totally on your own. A colleague with expertise in another field and interest in another industry can add a great deal to your strengths, offering a broader image to a wider marketplace. In the early 1980s, I lent my strategic planning experience and knowledge of the banking industry to a partnership with a fine Gonzaga Ph.D. knowledgeable in organizational behavior (OB) and the utilities industry. My bankers needed his OB skills and his utilities needed my strategic planning. Within 1 year we had developed a practice generating fees at the $1-million-a-year rate, yet neither of us could have done it on his own.

The Ethics of It All

Most professions have an ethic all their own. Consulting is no exception; however, without a codified body of knowledge or any national quality-control body like the AICPA for accounting, the ABA for lawyers, or the AMA for doctors, consulting is difficult to police or control. And I make this observation at a time in U.S. business when ethics and ethical behavior are more important than ever. Some colleges have both graduate and undergraduate courses in the subject. What, then, constitutes typical ethical dilemmas for consulting scholars? They appear to concentrate in four areas, and as with any discussion of ethics, there are no absolute answers, only what makes sense and seems right to the individual.

Conflicts With Academe. Some of the basic issues found here have to do with universities that have discrete policies about faculty consulting, from a limit on the number of hours you are permitted each month, to significant financial penalties in the form of tithing, up to 30% of your gross fees at some schools. The simple answer is that if the school knows what you are doing or provided the lead to the client for you, it is smart to play by the rules. However, I am aware of many colleagues who do not inform their schools or their colleagues about their consulting efforts and take the posture that what their school doesn't know won't hurt it. What they do on their own time is strictly their business. Okay by me, but I hope the administration never finds out. What is the price of tenure in this day and age? And what is your obligation to the university if they look the other way to allow you to consult as much as you want and even provide you with clients? Shouldn't you at least schedule your heavy consulting periods when you have no classes or during summer break? (I would rate this a two-beer, late-night discussion.)

Conflicts With Clients. When dealing with clients you may find errors of omission and commission. Errors of omission can be grave and include forgetting to ask for all the available data, not taking the time to do a thorough analysis before forming your hypotheses, and failing to include some executive or manager in your meetings because you do not like him or her personally. More in line with pure ethics are instances in which you uncover information of some danger to your client or sponsor or someone shares very sensitive information with you that ought to be passed on but that could cost the employee his or her job. Suppose the greatest barrier to the success of your client's firm is the CEO himself or herself? Do you tell the board or the executive committee? (A three-beer discussion, here.)

Errors of commission in this sector would include blatant favoritism to one manager or another, sharing sensitive data with people who ought not to know, colluding with senior management to lend your name to a report supporting precluded decisions and evaluations, excessively socializing with client executives of either sex, and accepting favors in exchange for sensitive data or preliminary observations. Agreeing to commit industrial espionage under the guise of research is another example (Each of these is worth a four-beer discussion. Suppose the espionage doesn't really hurt anyone —five beers! But if it has to do with trade secrets—six beers and call a cab!)

This is an increasingly tricky area. While you are waiting for the cab to come, try these: Would you work for a tobacco company? What do you do if you discover that your client is a major polluter? A firm with discriminatory policies? Your sponsor or the CEO is lying to you or withholding information?

Conflicts With Yourself. Your client shows you an internal company research report someone else did that is vital to research you are working on at school. No one will ever make the connection. Do you make and keep a copy? Your client shows you an extraordinarily professional report done by another consulting firm. Do you make and keep a copy? You are working for a company and are asked to perform similar work for a competitor for more money. Do you drop the first client, bowing out gracefully? How many personal long-distance calls should you make on the client's phone? (Each of the above is a one-beer discussion.) Should you tell a prospective client that you are a Ph.D. if you haven't finished your thesis? If a client has given you confidential data about a competitor's weaknesses, would you use that data to make a proposal to the competitor to correct the flaws? Would you tell a client that you finished a $30,000 contract with only $25,000 or would you bill the last $5,000 on the contract after the work is completed? You experience a $5,000 cost overrun. Do you eat it or tell the client it was his or her organization's fault and try to bill it back? A prospective client asks you about the consulting capability of one of your colleagues at school who also is bidding on this project. (Each is a three-beer discussion.)

Conflicts With Colleagues or Staff. This last area pertains to errors of omission or commission created by your colleagues with whom you are consulting. It might have been a friend you subcontracted something to or it might be a full-time professional in a firm you have an alliance with and you observe something that makes you feel uncomfortable. Do you confront the individual? Do you mention it to the client or to the partner of the firm with whom you have an alliance? To what extent are you responsible for the acts of others? If you say nothing, does that make you an accessory to unethical behavior? (Here it'll take four beers.)

All of the above represent but the tip of the ethics iceberg to be found in consulting. One of the silent stresses of consulting on your own is that the only policy is that which you make for yourself, and the only quality control is that which you apply to yourself. But in the end, you are the only one who has to live with yourself!

Summary and Conclusions

We started out about 130 pages ago, you and I, to discuss how you might take your scholarship and learned expertise and become a consultant to the private sector or government. What you have learned, I hope, is that the process of consultation is very complex, is very dependent on marketing and selling skills, and is only what you make of it.

Suggested Readings

Belmont, H. (1983). *Psychological strategies for success in consulting*. Washington, DC: Consultants Library.

Block, P. (1981). *Flawless consulting: A guide to getting your expertise used*. Austin, TX: Learning Concepts.

Cody, T. G. (1986). *Management consulting: A game without chips*. Fitzwilliam, NH: Kennedy.

Cohen, A. (1985). *How to make it big as a consultant*. New York: AMACOM.

Conner, R. A., & Davidson, J. P. (1985). *Marketing your consulting and professional services*. New York: Wiley.

Conner, R. A., & Davidson, J. P. (1987). *Getting new clients*. New York: Wiley.

Fox, J. A., & Levin, J. (1993). *Working with the media*. Newbury Park, CA: Sage.

Goldsmith, C. (1985). *Selling skills for CPAs: How to bring in new business*. New York: McGraw-Hill.

Greiner, L. E., & Metzger, R. O. (1982). *Consulting to management: Insights to building and managing a successful practice*. Englewood Cliffs, NJ: Prentice-Hall.

Hartmann, C. C. (1987). *100 tips on marketing and selling your consulting and professional services*.

Holtz, H. (1983). *How to suceed as an independent consultant*. New York: Wiley.

Kelly, K. (1989). *How to set your fees and get them*. Larchmont, NY: Visibility Enterprises.

Kennedy, J. H. (1982). *The news release idea book for management consultants*. Fitzwilliam, NH: Kennedy.

Kennedy, J. H. (Ed.). (1984). *25 "best" proposals by management consulting firms*. Fitzwilliam, NH: Kennedy.

Kennedy, J. H. (1988). *The management consulting idea book*. Fitzwilliam, NH: Kennedy.

Kishel, G., & Kishel, P. (1985). *Cashing in on the consulting boom.* New York: Wiley.

Kotler, P., & Bloom, P. N. (1984). *Marketing professional services.* Englewood Cliffs, NJ: Prentice-Hall.

Kubr, M. (Ed.). (1986). *Management consulting: A guide to the profession* (2nd ed.). Geneva: International Labor Organization.

Leavitt, H. J. (1978). *Managerial psychology.* Chicago: University of Chicago Press.

Lippitt, G. L. (1978). *Helping across cultures.* Washington, DC: International Consultants Foundation.

Lippett, G., & Lippett, R. (1986). *The consulting process in action.* Boston: University Associates.

Metzger, R. O. (1989). *Profitable consulting: Guiding America's managers into the next century.* Reading, MA: Addison-Wesley.

Moore, G. L. (1984). *The politics of management consulting.* New York: Praeger.

Quay, J. (1986). *Diagnostic interviewing for consultants and auditors.* Published by author.

Schein, E. H. (1969). *Process consultation: Its role in organizational development.* Reading, MA: Addison-Wesley.

Shenson, H. (1990). *Shenson on consulting.* New York: Wiley.

Sloane, C. S. (1986). The road ahead for consulting. *Journal of Management Consulting, 3,* 1.

Sonnenberg, F. K. (1990). *Marketing to win.* New York: HarperCollins.

Steele, F. (1982). *The role of the internal consultant.* Boston: CBI.

Tierno, D. A. (1986, Winter). Growth strategies for consulting in the next decade. *Sloan Management Review.*

Weinberg, G. M. (1986). *The secrets of consulting.* New York: Dorset.